DAPHNE DU MAURIER
AT HOME

Hilary Macaskill

DAPHNE DU MAURIER AT HOME

FRANCES LINCOLN LIMITED
PUBLISHERS

Frances Lincoln Limited
Aurum Publishing Group
74–77 White Lion Street
Islington, London N1 9PF
www.franceslincoln.com

Daphne du Maurier at Home
Copyright © Frances Lincoln Limited 2013
Text copyright © Hilary Macaskill 2013
Illustrations copyright as listed on page 144
First Frances Lincoln edition 2013

A catalogue record for this book is available
from the British Library.

ISBN 9-780-7112-3372-0

Printed and bound in China

9 8 7 6 5 4 3 2 1

PAGE 1 Daphne at Menabilly in
'trespassing days'.
PAGE 2 Daphne in the hall at
Menabilly, looking at the bust of her
father, Gerald. The walking sticks
were his; the arrows belonged to her
husband, Tommy.
RIGHT Fowey from Hall Walk in
Bodinnick.

Contents

FOREWORD

TESSA

I was born in Cannon Hall Cottage, Hampstead, the house in which Daphne and Tommy, my mother and father, lived when first married. It was attached to the garden of Cannon Hall, my grandparents' home, where Daphne and her sisters spent their teenage years. Sadly, my grandfather, Gerald du Maurier, died some months after I was born and the house was sold; my grandmother, Muriel, and my aunts, Angela and Jeanne, moved into the cottage. I have fond pre-war memories of staying there, being taken for the first time to see *Peter Pan* and studiously avoiding my grandmother's snappy Pekingese dogs.

In 2011 the Heath and Hampstead Society decided that Cannon Hall Cottage, now two houses, should have a plaque saying that my mother Daphne had lived there. I was asked to unveil it, which was a great pleasure and a small family occasion. We were warmly asked by one of the current owners if we would like to come inside and I was amused to see the room in which I was born.

Recently, through a friend of my daughter, I found myself invited to see Cannon Hall itself. This was a great thrill as, although we had pictures of the house, gardens and interiors, none of us had ever been inside. My daughter and I were met by the charming present-day owners, who showed us all over. We were delighted to find the house had not been altered, apart from obvious and necessary modernization, and was furnished in very good taste. My mother and grandparents could have walked in and felt immediately at home. What a joy it has been to find my mother's previous homes so well looked after and loved. Hilary Macaskill's splendid book has enhanced that feeling.

FLAVIA

This captivating book has awakened many fond memories of Menabilly, the house my mother rented in Cornwall. My first sight of Mena was when Daphne took us trespassing in the grounds of the then empty, forlorn building. We children were astonished to find the house covered in ivy, like a vast green shroud, no windows visible. My mother put out her hands and buried them in thick leaves while leaning her cheek against the hidden wall and kissing it. 'My house of secrets,' she said, her blue eyes lighting up with joy.

The family moved into Menabilly in 1943 and for me it was to be the best period of my life. My love for the house went very deep, and that was something I was able to share with my mother. Hilary Macaskill explores my mother's thoughts concerning different aspects of Menabilly, which featured in the books she wrote, and I am sure those who read this book will gain a new insight into Daphne's life.

Daphne made Menabilly into a place full of enchantment. In spring and early summer the house would be full of blood-red rhododendrons and pale pink and white camellias, placed in deep vases throughout the rooms. These flowers grew in splendid profusion in the lovely grounds.

In my mind's eye, I can still walk through all the rooms at Menabilly and place every picture on the walls and the furniture in the many rooms. Best of all is to linger at the end of the vast lawn and look back to Menabilly in all her glory.

KITS

My first memories of Ferryside – the house by the river Fowey, which my mother's family bought as a holiday home – are fragmentary. I can see my grandmother's face, stained with tears, looking out of the door. Her small Pekingese had died and she was heartbroken. These dogs were always part of the house, and as a small boy I lived in dread of them. They did not care for children, and whenever Gran bent to kiss me, the jealous little brutes would charge my ankles, nipping and snapping ferociously.

Gran seemed a rather formidable lady, but she became very deaf. Home from school for all-too-brief holidays, I would climb the stairs with my sisters and we would rather struggle to have meaningful conversations. Now, having lived at Ferryside for twenty years, there are so many things I would like to have talked to her about. She had a great gift for interior decorating and design: it was her creative talent that transformed a broken-down boatyard into a beautiful and loving home. I remember the house always had an elegant atmosphere and was full of flowers. I can still see the brilliant blue hydrangeas on the piano and sense the faint aroma of Narcissus Noir, Gran's favourite perfume.

My mother always loved Ferryside. Hilary Macaskill describes how she, together with my grandmother and my aunts, Angela and Jeanne, first discovered it, in the village of Bodinnick. It was here Daphne wrote her first novel, *The Loving Spirit*. On my visits there with my mother we would walk up the old path to the little greenhouse which overlooked the harbour and she would point out the boats below and tell me how she was filled with a terrific sense of joy at the prospect of her family living here and the freedom she felt after being in London. I feel certain she would be delighted that it is now my home.

It is well known that places and especially houses meant more to my mother than almost anything, apart from her family, and this book describes her homes and the profound influence they had upon her – and which, indeed, were the inspiration for so much of her writing.

LEFT Daphne's children, Flavia, Kits and Tessa, at Readymoney Cove in Fowey.
BELOW Flavia, Kits and Tessa, at Ferryside.

CHAPTER 1
A CHILDHOOD IN LONDON

After a night of thunderstorms in London, Daphne du Maurier was born on 13 May 1907 in a Nash terrace house overlooking Regent's Park. It seems a fitting place for a family that was used to the limelight. Daphne's grandfather, George du Maurier, had carved out an illustrious career as a cartoonist for the magazine *Punch* before turning to writing fiction and creating in *Trilby*, his best-selling second novel, a character whose name, Svengali, has entered the English language (as well as giving, in its title, the name to a new style of hat). Daphne's father, Gerald, had become a professional actor in 1894.

By the time of Daphne's birth, the family fortunes were good. The previous year Gerald du Maurier had played the title role in *Raffles, The Amateur Cracksman*, a play based on the series of books by E.W. Hornung about a gentleman thief. Gerald played him to perfection, the play had a long run, and he was ready to move up in the world. In 1903, he had married Muriel Beaumont, with whom he had fallen in love when they had both acted in *The Admirable Crichton*, a James Barrie play at the Duke

Daphne in the summer of 1930, the year she finished her first novel, *The Loving Spirit*.

of York's Theatre, and they had set up home in a small house in nearby Chester Place, where their first daughter Angela was born, in 1904.

The family's new home, 24 Cumberland Terrace, was not only bigger but also more distinguished. Hidden behind an arch, in the corner of a courtyard, and with steps leading up to the front door, it was set in the largest of the terraces built by John Nash, after being commissioned in 1811 by George IV when he was Prince Regent; its facade was adorned with fluted columns and pediments filled with sculpture. Cumberland Terrace was the first house that mattered to Daphne. Near the end of her life when she was considering writing *Growing Pains: The Shaping of a Writer* (later retitled as *Myself When Young*), she had the strong feeling that she should base it on the houses she had known and the influence they had on her development, starting with her birthplace – which 'I remember very vividly'.

In her own memoir *It's Only the Sister*, Angela reported that their mother said Daphne was 'the loveliest tiny baby she has ever seen'. This early approbation appears not to have continued, for there was, as Daphne herself wrote, a lack of attachment between her and her mother: she was to become much closer to her father.

Daphne was christened at Christ Church in nearby Albany Street. (Perhaps the name was Gerald's suggestion: he had been briefly engaged to the actress Ethel Daphne Barrymore, whom he called Daphne.) In those early days, according to Angela, Daphne was taken around Regent's Park in 'a beautiful white pram, which matched our white front door'. Four years later, in 1911, Jeanne, the youngest sister, was born; one of Daphne's earliest memories is of excursions with the baby in the pram, along Broad Walk, bordering the zoo, or sometimes into Park Square Gardens, enclosed by railings with entrance only by a key.

With high ceilings and large windows looking out over the trees and flower beds of Regent's Park, their home was quite a grand residence. But what Daphne remembered best was the sanctuary of the nursery – with a doll's house, a toy cupboard with one shelf for Angela and one for her, a cretonne-covered toy box and an old armchair that could play the part of a ship wrecked at sea. The nursery was over their parents' bedroom (the children had to be quiet in the mornings, as Gerald slept late), with a view of rooftops and over Albany Street barracks, where the regiment of the Royal Horse Guards was then stationed: the bugles of Reveille and the Last Post were regular accompaniments to the children's rising and sleeping rituals. Sometimes, thrillingly, the soldiers could be seen riding their horses to or from the barracks, in full gleaming and plume-nodding regalia.

The nursery too was the site of many impromptu performances of *Peter Pan*, a play with particular connections to the du Mauriers. James Barrie had been a close friend of Gerald's sister Sylvia and her husband, Arthur Llewellyn Davies, having first seen their sons playing together in Kensington Gardens when he and his wife

ABOVE Daphne's grandfather, the author and cartoonist George du Maurier.
LEFT Daphne's parents, Muriel and Gerald du Maurier.
RIGHT Muriel and Gerald with Daphne, on the left, and her sisters: Jeanne, the youngest, in the middle and Angela, the oldest, on the right.

DAPHNE DU MAURIER AT HOME

ABOVE This portrait of Muriel was taken before she gave up acting in 1910.
OPPOSITE Daphne outside her birthplace, 24 Cumberland Terrace, Regent's Park.

decades, as he reprised the role many times. Barrie, long-standing friend of Gerald's family too (he was known as 'Uncle Jim'), would often visit and the children would act out this favourite of plays: play-acting was something that they all did, especially Daphne. 'Daphne always bagged Peter,' remembered Angela, while she was Wendy and Mrs Darling. The vision of them swooping from chair to chair, swimming as mermaids on the floor or in combat with their father as Captain Hook, while Barrie sat by the fire watching them, is a potent one, and emblematic of the theatrical household.

And it was, inevitably, a household dominated by the theatre. Muriel had continued to act for a while – she played Nerissa in *The Merchant of Venice* and in a number of French comedies – but she gave up the stage in 1910. The following year, after Jeanne was born, Muriel turned her complete attention to her family and to supporting Gerald in his escalating career in the theatre. With his sleek good looks and a casual confidence that stemmed from his position as the precious and cherished youngest child of his family – he had four sisters and an older brother – he had become a matinee idol. He was immensely popular, and he was talented. He initiated a form of naturalistic acting that led some critics to dismiss him as just being 'always himself', which – as Daphne pointed out in her biography of him – was unjust. He was capable of considerable range, sometimes to the inconvenience of the family: Daphne wrote of how he would totally inhabit his part, so that if he was playing Bulldog Drummond, he was gay and light-hearted at home as well as on stage; when in the role of the troubled character Will Dearth, in *Dear Brutus*, another Barrie play, he was sad and tormented. But in his own skin, he had enormous charm, which he worked on his family, and which was also an invaluable asset in his other burgeoning career, in theatre management. In 1910, he went into partnership with theatre manager Frank Curzon, and, backed by Curzon's financial acumen, managed Wyndham's Theatre for fifteen years, before moving on to St James's Theatre. Later, he became President of

were walking with their dog Porthos (coincidentally named after the dog in George du Maurier's first novel *Peter Ibbetson*), and Barrie wrote *Peter Pan* with them in mind. In the first production in 1904, Gerald played the evil Captain Hook and also the part of the benevolent Mr Darling – an innovative doubling up suggested by actor rather than playwright that has become traditional. Captain Hook was a part that was associated with Gerald for

DAPHNE DU MAURIER AT HOME

the Actors' Orphanage Fund, ensuring that the annual garden party became a highlight of the social calendar, and in 1922 he was knighted.

With his role in the spotlight – at work and at home – it is not surprising that family life revolved around Gerald, and his roles. As the youngest child he had been indulged by his parents and siblings, and this indulgence continued in his own family circle. Since, however, he had a great sense of fun, this was not a hardship. In keeping with his career in entertainment, he needed to be entertained, so their family life was augmented by constant social activities, when they fitted in with his work.

Gerald's whims ruled the daily life of the family – and the holidays. One year, when he stopped working for a spell, they adjourned to Wales, to Llanbedr in Snowdonia, a house filled with relatives and friends, while the children, to their glee, stayed in a cottage at the end of the garden. The family took holidays in Dinard and Dieppe. But they also, from May to August, had summer homes in countryside close to London. One in particular left a lasting impression on Daphne: Slyfield Manor, an Elizabethan mansion near Cobham in Surrey that was rather scary at night-time, when she had to climb the broad staircase alone on her way to bed; but with its large grounds, the river Mole running through the garden and a farm next door, there were endless opportunities for play-acting. There, she became Christian in *The Pilgrim's Progress*, the muddied fields standing in for the Slough of Despond and the river Mole the River of Death.

Other summer homes were at Denham in Buckinghamshire, Croxley Green in Hertfordshire and Cookham in Berkshire. In 1915, the family lived for a while in Chorley Wood on the border of Hertfordshire and Buckinghamshire, at Soulsbridge Cottage, which the du Mauriers bought after Gerald's mother died. Chorley Wood was already in the commuter belt, as the Metropolitan

Cannon Hall, the du Maurier family's home in Hampstead.

Railway had extended out here in 1889. For Gerald, however, the advantage was that he could drive in to the theatre (the family's fortunes were reflected in the fact that they had, by 1911, acquired two cars, a Rolls Royce and a Ford), but though it was within easy reach of London, it was still rural, still a village, noted for its common, then grazed by cattle. At Chorley Wood Daphne, at the age of eight, attained a measure of freedom, wandering across the fields with her first dog, a West Highland terrier called Jock. There was a lot of acting too: she had just read *Treasure Island* and so, with the willing support of Jeanne (Angela was now doing lessons), Daphne became Jim Hawkins and occasionally Long John Silver, while Jeanne was Blind Pew.

In this period Muriel too acquired a measure of independence, as she was taught how to drive, in a somewhat idiosyncratic manner: Gerald took her back to Regent's Park in a Studebaker, the car of the moment, had her drive twice round the relatively calm and secluded Outer Circle, and then left the car, telling her to drive back home. And so she did. 'As home at that moment was Chorley Wood, one staggers at the temerity of both of them,' wrote Angela.

Gerald inclined towards the countryside. At least, he thought he did. He was a keen birdwatcher, but as with all things, he did not want to stick at birdwatching for long, and the countryside did not offer as much diversion as the town. In 1916 Gerald decided he must move back to his roots in Hampstead. He looked for a house, almost settling on one that overlooked the White Stone Pond at the top of Heath Street. He longed to return to the home of his youth, New Grove House opposite Fenton House, in what is now Hampstead Grove, but instead bought Cannon Hall, a mansion behind high walls, very close to Hampstead Heath. Described in *The Annals of Hampstead*, published in 1912, as 'a fine old Georgian red-brick house', it had been the home of Sir Noah Thomas, who was graced with the title of Physician-in-Ordinary to George III (a fact that would often be mentioned to

Gerald's guests). Cannon Hall stands on the corner of Cannon Place, its dull red brick walls winding down adjacent Squire's Mount and curving back along Well Road, ending in a pair of cottages at the bottom of the garden. Gerald was much taken with the paved courtyard with its central fountain and statue (no longer there) behind wrought-iron gates, and the hall with its fireplace and elegant staircase enhanced by carved barley-twist balusters provided a suitably superior entrance. It was a rambling

ABOVE AND RIGHT The large drawing room at Cannon Hall, originally two rooms, was filled with furniture enthusiastically bought by Gerald to suit the mid-Georgian period of the house.

house, with large living rooms, a balcony from the drawing room, a view over London from Gerald's bedroom that he adored and large nursery accommodation for the children: the night nursery, which Daphne and Jeanne shared, had its own bathroom and lavatory. 'This was promotion indeed,' Daphne thought.

She soon discovered that one of the windows led to a flat roof, from which she could reach the courtyard, but she was soon discovered doing this and forbidden from doing so again. 'A pity. It damped adventure.' Less contentious was her practice of waving each night from the night nursery window to the lighted window of a house at the back of the house opposite: years later, she found to her excitement that it had at that time been the home of her literary heroine, Katherine Mansfield.

The grounds of Cannon Hall were extensive: terrace, lawns, kitchen garden, fruit trees and greenhouses were all contained by the mellow wall. There was too (and still is) a small brick building with barred windows giving on to Squire's Mount that used to be the Hampstead Lock-up until 1832. Miscreants would spend the night there on a bed of straw before being marched up to the hall to receive justice. More mundanely, it was in 1916 used for storing coal and coke, but in the girls' childhood games it was restored to its original status.

Cannon Hall was altogether a desirable residence for a successful actor-manager, and new furniture of a suitable period was bought to enhance the rooms. It was a house where Gerald could be happy – and so his daughters could be too. Their life there quickly fell into a pattern: long walks across the heath from White Stone Pond, or along Spaniards Road; large Sunday lunches for the family and, later, for friends, including actresses Gladys Cooper – who became a particular friend of the whole family – and Viola Tree; games of cricket on the lawn with Daphne and Jeanne. In 1922, a hard tennis court was installed, and tennis parties were added to the social calendar.

It was fertile territory for an imaginative child. Angela reminisced about the game she and Daphne used to play where they were 'two strange women called Mrs Snow and Mrs Sheldon, and we had about twenty children each. Some of them were merely in our minds, some were our very precious teddy-bears, one of Daphne's was actually a piece of cork found on a beach, called Ruth.' Daphne was even then perceptive: Angela had been entranced by letters from fairies that she found in the garden when they were staying at Slyfield Manor, though Daphne, at the age of five, refused to be hoodwinked. But fantasy games were another matter. She was reading avidly, and Walter Scott novels and *The Three Musketeers* provided inspiration. Not surprisingly, in view of who her parents were, she began play-acting from a young age, developing an absorbing imaginary world. This focused for a couple of years in her early teens on the exploits of Eric Avon, captain of cricket at Rugby School, with 'one's dress tucked into one's knickers for a doublet, and a woollie over one's shoulders for a cape'.

The role of Eric Avon had, perhaps, a particular significance, for though Gerald held publicly to the belief that 'daughters are the thing' (a line he would quote from *Dear Brutus*), he seemed to yearn for a son. All his daughters had played cricket with their

Daphne, before she left for finishing school in France in 1925.

DAPHNE DU MAURIER AT HOME

father, but it was to Daphne that he wrote an extraordinary poem about being a boy: the first verse ends, 'And if I'd had my way/ She would have been a boy.' It was to Daphne he said, 'I wish I was your brother instead of your father; we'd have such fun.' Curiously, Eric Avon became Daphne's alter ego not long after the shock of menstruation beginning – perhaps it was bitter irony that led her to dub the month's visitation 'Robert', which became one of the code words used in the family. Such intensive play-acting meant that her alter ego remained with her all her life – she later referred to him as 'the 'boy-in-the-box'. In *Growing Pains*, she points to how Eric Avon remained in her unconscious, and how he emerged – though with very different characteristics – in her five novels with masculine narrators.

Daphne attended school for a while in Hampstead, at what is now St Margaret's, a small private establishment in Kidderpore Gardens (not surprisingly, one of the three houses is called Du Maurier). It had been started in 1884, and was known as Miss Tulloch's School, after the formidable Scottish ex-governess who set it up and ran it for forty-four years. When Daphne went there it was in Oak Hill Park, much closer – just a few minutes' walk away (it returned to Kidderpore Gardens after the Second World War). But school was an experiment that didn't last long. In 1918, Daphne's parents decided to again employ a governess. Maud Waddell, whom Angela and Daphne nicknamed Tod, was then in her early thirties. By Angela's account, she was a 'remarkable governess', teaching them history of art, French and English history, literature, mythology and geography. A close bond developed between Daphne and Tod that was to become a lifelong friendship.

At the end of 1920, Tod left to take up a glamorous position in Constantinople (now Istanbul), as a governess in the harem of what turned out to be the last Sultanate of the Ottoman Empire. The family implored her to change her mind. An ardent letter from Daphne, scrawled in pencil because she had 'Robert' and

was lying on the sofa, said, 'I miss you awfully, so I do hope you will be able to return,' before rattling on with local gossip and news – she was going to be in a tableau with Ellen Terry 'and my adorable Gladys' – and then laying plans for the future: 'I've got the most exquisite idea; when I am seventine [Tod claimed to have lost sleep because of Daphne's handwriting and spelling] it would be ripping if instead of going to Paris, you and I travelled in Italy . . . we could live in a Bohemian way (baths of course), talk French, and you do a lot of painting. I think I should take up writing or poetry!!'

Tod resisted Daphne's pleas to return, but a regular correspondence between them began, with Daphne giving details of everyday life and of holidays, which, as Gerald's stock rose, became more exotic: Cannes, Monte Carlo and seven weeks in Algiers at the Hotel St George with – excitingly – orange trees in the garden. Travelling *en famille* was a huge enterprise, especially with Gerald's predilections, staff and companions: 'travelling in the grand manner', as Daphne described it later, 'an experience not to be lightly undertaken'.

However, one significant holiday for Daphne was more local, at Mullion Cove in Cornwall, when she was five. In fact, although the whole family set out together, only the children remained there, in the charge of the nurse, the nursery maid and the then governess, for soon after their arrival Gerald, irritated by the rain, began pining for the social whirl and casino life of Dieppe, so Muriel, ever-indulgent, left the children with the servants and departed with him. One memorable night, the children were excitedly roused from their beds to witness a shoal of pilchards arriving in the cove, which filled Daphne with a 'wild delight'.

The family returned to Cornwall for another holiday when Daphne was ten, to a house near Kennack Sands, close to the Lizard. There in 'a pool set beneath the cliffs, mysterious and shallow, yet deep enough to cover a child's hips' she taught herself to swim. Swimming became a pastime that stayed

For all Gerald's bonhomie, his frolicking with his children became something different as his daughters grew up. 'He would have liked us all to be nuns, as long as Home remained the Convent,' wrote Angela succinctly. 'He would have had us all remain Peter Pans, we used to hear a lot about having "the bloom rubbed off" (which really meant he did not approve of his daughters being kissed).' He became censorious, especially, it seems, with Daphne. After she met Carol Reed (later to become a noted film director) when they were both guests of the crime writer Edgar Wallace and his family on a winter sports holiday in Switzerland, she started to spend a lot of time with him. When she was out late with him, Gerald would wait up for her and chastise her furiously.

For Daphne, the problem was more acute than with her sisters, as she had always had what Angela described as 'a special affinity' with her father. From an early age, she had been his companion on walks, his confidante. Gerald paid scant regard to the effect he had on his daughter, nor to his effect on others. He was in the habit of flirting. The family was well aware of Gerald's dalliances, and used to laugh about his 'stable' of young actresses. He would woo his leading ladies with lunches and trinkets such as diamond bracelets. The singer Gracie Fields in her autobiography described how impressed she was when, fresh from her cabaret at Talk of the Town in the West End, she received an engraved calling card from 'Sir Gerald du Maurier', with a note scribbled beneath: 'I would like to see you.' He wanted to try her out, he said, for the play he was producing. Dressed idiosyncratically in her 'favourite scarlet and emerald tartan kilt, my purple Hungarian blouse, my fur coat and my Scots tammy', she turned up for the rehearsal and, despite the nerves induced by Gladys Cooper and Tallulah Bankhead sitting in on the rehearsal, and despite Gerald giving her a 'long sloppy kiss' that wasn't in the script, she rose to the occasion. 'Doggedly I la-de-dahed my way through Lady Weir's lines.' And she got the part. It was her first straight acting job, and

with her as an important part of her routine in her adult life.

Another landmark holiday was in Thurlestone, in south Devon, when she was fourteen, as she described in *Growing Pains*. While there she felt the first frisson of sexual attraction – to her cousin Geoffrey, also an actor, who was twenty-two years older than her (and just twelve years younger than her father). There was nothing more than 'the holding of hands under the rug', and, above all, the knowledge that it must be secret, but it was a potent sensation. On the last day on the beach, when Geoffrey said goodbye to her, they looked up and saw her father staring down on them from the clifftop. It was an uncomfortable moment.

she acquitted herself well, but had to go along with the lunches and the attention Gerald paid her – though she put him in his place with 'Ee lad, don't be soft, you're older than my Dad!' These were cutting words for a man who longed to remain young: his eyes, she said, filled with tears. It was perhaps as much from realization of his own ageing that Gerald hated his daughters growing up and away from him.

But Daphne left, going away to finishing school in France in 1925. She wrote ecstatically to Tod about Paris, 'its cobbled streets and shrieking taxis', the chic little women and – with a perhaps unconscious nod to her grandfather – the 'men with

OPPOSITE Cousin Geoffrey, an actor, during rehearsals at Wyndham's Theatre.
ABOVE Jeanne, Angela and Daphne in the conservatory at Cannon Hall.

broad-brimmed Trilby hats'. She visited Versailles, the Louvre and Fontainebleau – 'I adored them all' – as well as the Place de la Concorde, especially 'at night, after it's been raining'.

Her first impressions of her finishing school, though, were

rather jolting. For a start she was expected to make her own bed – something she refused to do, persuading another pupil to do it for her. Fresh from the comforts of Cannon Hall, she found the cold and the discomfort unbearable. But what made it all bearable eventually was a charismatic teacher, Fernande Yvon, who captivated Daphne. She told Tod how she'd 'quite fallen' for her. 'She has a fatal attraction . . . She's absolutely kind of turned me on and now I'm coiled up in the net!' Behaving in a way that might not be viewed with such equanimity today, Mlle Yvon often, according to Daphne, 'pops up to the bedroom at odd moments'. The intense teenage crush turned into friendship, and Daphne, smitten as much by Paris and France as by this very grown-up relationship – and with the blessing of her parents – holidayed with Ferdy, as she became known, frequently in the next few years, and remained in touch with her until her death in 1965.

Part of the attraction of Daphne's trips to France was her desire to escape Hampstead. Her urge to write, which she had expressed to Tod when she was fourteen, continued not only for its own sake but also to make some money, so that she could become independent of the family. She made desultory attempts to settle down to writing poetry and short stories – first in a loggia by the tennis court, and later in the room over the garage. She showed some to her father, who was enthusiastic: he thought she had some of the skill of his father. But she felt herself often being distracted by the pleasures of life; any excuse served to put her efforts aside, especially the chance to go to films, plays or operas. She was endlessly dissatisfied both with her efforts and with life in London. It seemed impossible to move forward.

More and more, she planned trips to France. In the year she was nineteen, she spent the summer in Brittany with Ferdy at Trébeurden, 'a glorious spit, with an almost deserted beach beneath our hotel windows'. Daphne swam, walked and climbed the cliffs – and planned her future life and work, meditating on where she would make her home: 'The sea must be close, there had to be sea.' The wildness and isolation of Brittany thrilled her, and fuelled her creativity. She read Voltaire and Maupassant and began to write a short story, 'La Sainte Vierge', set in a Breton village, of a deceived wife who is unable to see what is going on in front of her – perhaps reflecting her own observations. After six weeks on the Brittany coast, she was full of dreams of the sort of place she would live and write in. Perhaps an island. Perhaps Greece . . .

But when she arrived home at the end of August, Muriel announced that there was a plan to look for a holiday home. Gerald had recently produced and helped adapt (by changing much of the dialogue) *The Ringer*, the first play by the prolific novelist Edgar Wallace, which had been a huge success (When it was later published as a novel, Wallace dedicated it to Gerald: 'Herein you will find all the improvements you suggested.') Wallace had been generous, insisting that Gerald have half the profits, so there was money to spare. Gerald and Muriel, partly impelled by the desire for a holiday home where Gerald could relax, but also perhaps prompted by the prospect of finding somewhere to tempt Daphne away from France, whence she was fleeing at every opportunity, thought of buying a house in Cornwall. Daphne remembered with affection Mullion Cove and Kennack Sands. But just now, full of energy and bursting with ideas after her French sojourn, she wanted to write; in fact, the room over the garage at Cannon Hall, her writing den, was the only place she wanted to be. Muriel, however, was determined that Daphne accompany her, as well as Angela and Jeanne, and Daphne agreed that she would relish some sea air. This trip was to change her life.

Gerald in the courtyard of Cannon Hall by the statue he cherished.

CHAPTER 2
FREEDOM AT FERRYSIDE

In the middle of September 1926, the du Maurier sisters and their mother took the train from Paddington to Cornwall, to Looe. No one seemed quite sure why Looe was fixed on as the destination, apart from the fact that it was on the coast. Angela wrote that she could not remember why it was chosen and, once there, 'we certainly could not imagine why'. Their first night in Cornwall was clearly restless: 'throughout our first and only night there, the village clock chimed every quarter and kept us all awake in the small commercial hotel'. By breakfast time, they had unanimously concluded that Looe was out of the question. So Muriel hired a car and a driver to take them further round the coast to Fowey. It was a beautiful drive along country lanes: far away to the north were the green and brooding expanses of Bodmin Moor (later to provide significant inspiration for Daphne) and, to the south, cliffs falling away to the sea. In the last mile or so, the road wound down to sea level, hugging the edge of the river Fowey, and ended at the small settlement of Bodinnick-by-Fowey. Many years later, in *Vanishing Cornwall*, written when she was nearly sixty, Daphne recalled the joy of that moment:

The hired car swept round the curve of the hill and suddenly the full expanse of Fowey harbour was spread beneath us. The contrast between this sheet of wide water, the nearby jetties, the moored ships, the grey roofs of Fowey across the way, the clustering cottages of Polruan on the opposite hill by the harbour mouth, and narrow, claustrophobic Looe where we had spent the night was astonishing, like the gateway to another world. My spirits soared.

There, by the ferry that continually plied back and forth across the river between Bodinnick and Fowey, as one had for seven centuries, they discharged the car and its driver. It was lunchtime, and rather than immediately crossing to Fowey, they turned left to climb the steep main street to the Ferry Inn. It was an auspicious decision, for it was then that they saw a 'For Sale' sign on a gate just by the ferry. After lunch, while Muriel talked to the landlord about their quest over coffee, the three sisters slipped away and back to the 'For Sale' sign.

Beyond the sign was a house squeezed in between the hillside and the river: 'a strange-looking house, built like a Swiss chalet'. The ferryman told them it was called Swiss Cottage. To urban sophisticates of Hampstead, where 'Swiss Cottage' was just down

Fowey harbour, with Gribbin Head in the background.

the Finchley Road and, moreover, the name of a London Underground station, the name was unpromising. But the ramshackle building, basically a boatyard with a loft above and rooms for living at the top, immediately won their hearts.

In her diary that night Daphne wrote: 'Bang on the river is the most divine little house for sale, which we all go mad about and want at once. M will see the owner tomorrow.' In *Vanishing Cornwall*, she filled in the background. While Angela and Jeanne tried the gate by the ferry and went into the yard, Daphne, independent as ever, found another gate leading round the back of the building to what passed for a garden: tiers of terraces steeply rising to Hall Walk, a broad bridleway that passed along the top of the hill. The building backed into the cliff, seemingly into the rock, while the river was directly in front, with a stream running through the middle of the yard beneath the building.

The car ferry at Bodinnick, as it was in the 1950s.

Standing at the river's edge and gazing up-river and down to the estuary and the sea, Daphne was entranced by the boats, the yachts, the ferry – and the ship that was being drawn by tugs, ready to moor before moving up-river to the china clay works. 'There was a smell in the air of tar and rope and rusted chain, a smell of tidal water. Down harbour, round the point was the open sea. Here was the freedom I desired, long sought-for, not yet known. Freedom to write, to walk, to wander, freedom to climb hills, to pull a boat, to be alone.' She said, all those years later, that when she was standing there, absorbing this atmosphere, marvelling at the chance discovery of this place, she remembered a line from a forgotten book, 'where a lover looks for the first time

upon his chosen one – "I for this, and this for me."'

Daphne and her sisters had decided. It seems that Muriel needed little persuasion, for the house was bought the following week. Their search for a holiday home was over.

Fowey was to become the focus of the family. Compared to Bodinnick, it was a teeming metropolis. It now has just 2,000 inhabitants, but it is still a thriving port with an illustrious history, which sent ships to join the battle against the Spanish Armada. The centuries-old china clay trade remains part of the local industry. Huge ships escorted by tugs can still be seen gliding up-river to the clay works, though there are not so many now.

Ferryside seen from the top of the terraced garden. On the other side of the river are the jetties of the china clay works.

FOWEY
the centre of the
CORNISH RIVIERA

MABEL
LUCIE
ATTWELL

When Queen Victoria and Prince Albert visited in 1846 during a yachting cruise, the Queen wrote in her diary that Fowey was 'situated in a creek very much like Dartmouth and is very pretty'. They landed at Broad Slip, later renamed the Victoria and Albert Quay, and drove through 'some of the narrowest streets I ever saw in England, and up perpendicular hills in the streets; it really quite alarmed me.'

The poet Robert Bridges called Fowey 'the most poetic-looking place in England'. James Barrie wrote to the Dutch novelist Maarten Maartens, 'it is but a toy town to look at on a bay so small hemmed in so picturesquely by cliffs and ruins that, of a moonlight night, it might pass for a scene in a theatre.' Fowey, with its cascade of pastel-coloured cottages, has attracted

ABOVE Mabel Lucie Attwell's drawings illustrated this publicity booklet produced later by the Chamber of Commerce. The introduction was by Daphne.
OPPOSITE The Q Memorial to Sir Arther Quiller-Couch – author, academic and mentor to Daphne – at Penleath Point, overlooking his beloved Fowey estuary.

artists and writers, from Mabel Lucie Attwell, whose illustrations of chubby children adorned many children's books in the early twentieth century, to James Barrie and Kenneth Grahame, who splashed about on the river Fowey and, it is said, modelled Toad Hall in *Wind in the Willows* on Fowey Hall – now Fowey Hall Hotel. He was a friend, as was James Barrie, of Fowey's most important literary resident, Sir Arthur Quiller-Couch, who is thought to have been Grahame's model for the character of the talkative Water Rat, who tells his friend the Mole that 'there is nothing – absolutely nothing – half so much worth doing as simply messing about in boats', as was very much Sir Arthur's view. He would row across the river to his garden, below Hall Walk, near which is now the striking granite memorial to him, inscribed 'Great Cornishman. Writer. Scholar.' Though 'Q', as he was known, is most remembered as the first editor of *The Oxford Book of English Verse,* he was also the author of a series of best-selling books about Fowey (which he called Troy) and its characters. The small yachts with their brightly coloured sails that dart about the harbour in twice-weekly races between May and September are named Troys in his honour. In the first of these engaging books, *The Astonishing History of Troy Town*, he describes Fowey (Troy), Polruan (Penpoodle) and Boddinick (which has a book all of its own, *The Shining Ferry*):

> Here is a lovely harbour flanked by bold hills to right and to left; here are the ruined castles, witnesses of the great days when Troy sent ships to Agincourt; here are grey houses huddled at the water's edge, hoary battered walls, and quay-doors coated with ooze and green weed. Such is Troy, and on the further shore quaint Penpoodle faces us, where a silver creek runs up to Lanbeg. Further up, the harbour melts into a river where the old ferry-boat plies to and from the foot of a tiny village straggling up the hill; further yet, and the jetties mingle with the steep woods beside the road, where the vessels lie thickest, ships of all builds and of all nations, from the trim Canadian timber-ship to the corpulent Billy-boy. Why, the very heart of the picturesque is here. What more can you want?!

The book is a hymn to the Troy River (which he grandiloquently likens to the Rhine) and to the Trojan picnic, which is 'no ordinary function'. It was, Q explained, essentially patriotic – devoted to the cult of the Troy River – and so there would be a solemn procession:

> Undeviating tradition has fixed its goal at a sacred rock, haunted of heron and kingfisher, and wrapped around with woodland, beside a creek so tortuous as to simulate a series of enchanted lakes. Here the self-respecting Trojan, as his boat cleaved the solitude, will ask his fellows earnestly and at regular intervals whether they ever beheld anything more lovely; and they, in duty bound and absolute truthfulness, will answer that they never did.

It's a sentiment with which the du Mauriers would have

whole-heartedly concurred, for as Angela wrote in her diary they had fallen 'in love with Fowey directly'. Muriel lost no time in contacting local workmen and, demonstrating her great flair for interior design and practical adjustments, transformed the ex-boatyard into the idiosyncratic and comfortable home that it is today. Staircases were built, ceilings were lowered, bathrooms were added, oak was 'pickled' (stained in a light colour). The spot of the actual boatyard became a magnificent long room built against the rock with a widely arched window overlooking the river, and views down the harbour to the sea beyond. The house was renamed Ferryside.

Twenty years later, this room provided the setting for Daphne's play *September Tide*, when it became 'Stella Martyn's house on a Cornish estuary'. The set designer went to Ferryside and reproduced it exactly, even to the stable-type door. 'The room of stone and timber is long and low and is built against the living rock, of which part can be seen. From time to time the sounds of ships' sirens are heard along with the lap of water at high tide and the cries of gulls.' The all-important Ferry Inn, which caused the du Mauriers to discover Ferryside, makes its appearance on the front page of the play and in the last scene.

The loft above, with its smaller shuttered windows, was turned

into bedrooms. Daphne was delighted to find that the bedroom she and Jeanne would share had a door into one level of the garden. The top floor, once a separate flat, became everyday living rooms and a kitchen, also with a door leading out into the garden. The house was painted pale yellow with green windows and shutters. Nowadays, the smart white and blue-trimmed house remains a distinctive du Maurier landmark, as Kits Browning, Daphne's son, is the third generation of du Mauriers to live there.

Once the alterations were completed, all was ready for inspection by Gerald. At the quayside there was even a motor boat, freshly painted and named *Cora Ann* after the heroine in *The*

OPPOSITE AND ABOVE Ferryside, as transformed in 1927 by Daphne's mother, Muriel, and as it is today, now the home of Daphne's son, Kits, and his wife, Hacker.

Ringer – a nod to Edgar Wallace, who had made this all possible. One can imagine Gerald's arrival, with the family hovering about him, anxiously awaiting his approval. It was granted – though he added, 'I should like to get some dynamite and blow up those houses opposite, with grey roofs' – and the ancient boatyard became a distinctive holiday home for the family.

They came down for the summer months, and, in keeping with their sociability, invited many friends down to share their Cornwall hideaway. One was Viola Tree, who arrived by launch, missed her step on to the quay and fell into the harbour. 'She swam round in circles calling out, "Lovely, lovely" and emerged at last, a dripping curious figure, picture hat a little askew, and satin skirt covered in straw and mackerel scales.' On another occasion, according to Angela, Gracie Fields, with her manager and husband Archie Pitt, turned up at Ferryside, where Gracie did cartwheels on the lawn, rowed out to the harbour point singing at the top of her voice and returned to the house to make a 'fabulous offer' for it which, 'I'm thankful to say, was refused.'

Popular though it was with the du Maurier family, as a whole, as a summer home – and occasional Christmas sojourn – it was on Daphne that Ferryside worked its magic. On the day after her twentieth birthday, she was left alone there when the family returned to London. 'I was on my own for the first time in my life. A Mrs Coombs came in to cook, but that didn't count. I was free, I could come and go as I pleased, when I pleased.'

She threw herself into seaside life, learning to sail and to fish.

Harry Adams, who was skipper of *Cora Ann*, taught her to do both. She got to know the neighbours, including the Hunkins, who had a boatyard. She knew very quickly that 'this was my place, these were my people'. She was soon well recognized by 'her' people, who saw her coming from the railway station (Fowey was then on a loop line from Par to Lostwithiel, but the line closed in 1965), which was next to the river, to catch the ferry to Ferryside, a thrill that never palled as she stood on the quay and shouted 'Over'. It was a taste of freedom. 'I could come down to Fowey, do what I liked and pay for myself.'

She wrote to Tod that she disliked leaving: she felt this was her home, and hated to be anywhere else. She confided in her diary: 'I think Fowey means more to me than anything now. The river, the harbour, the sea. It's much more than love for a person.' Daphne began exploring, starting the habit of long walks which was to be so much a part of her life.

On one of her excursions, she found herself by Pont Pill, the tidal creek that leads off the Fowey River between Bodinnick and Polruan. Nowadays, it is charmingly populated with yachts, their sails furled, waiting for their owners to come and enjoy their weekend leisure in the Fowey estuary and out at sea. Then, it was something of a boat graveyard, where broken ships waited to be mended or abandoned. And there, one day, she found a wrecked schooner, the *Jane Slade*, with a carved figurehead. It caught her imagination, and even more so when she asked Adams about it and he told her that his wife was the granddaughter of the original Jane Slade, the widow who had run the family business: the schooner named after her was built in the family's Polruan yard, and for fifty years had traded out of Fowey.

Daphne spent that Christmas there with the family and other relatives, including her cousin Geoffrey, who tried to stroke her knees under the table (she called him her Borgia brother), and though the chimney smoked in the living room and there were problems with the kitchen boiler, Christmas was deemed a great

OPPOSITE The sitting room at Ferryside. Its back wall was built into the cliff.
ABOVE Pont Pill, the sheltered tidal creek where Daphne found the wreck of *Jane Slade*, the story of which inspired her first novel, *The Loving Spirit*.

success. Afterwards, the family packed up and went back to London, but Daphne stayed on and started work: 'No garage-room at Cannon Hall, but my own bedroom with a flat desk facing the window and the harbour.' She was working on a story called 'The Doll' (only recently rediscovered, and published in 2011). She was still writing poetry and short stories; two ('And Now to God the Father', about a social-climbing vicar, and 'A Difference in Temperament', about the disintegration of a relationship) were bought by *The Bystander* magazine and eventually published in the summer of 1929.

On Daphne's twenty-first birthday, Muriel bought her a rowing boat, painted black, named *Annabelle Lee*, with 'a little red sail to go with her, just to hoist before the wind.' But best of all a sailing boat, the *Marie-Louise* (the name of her aunt May), was being built for her at Polruan boatyard – the same boatyard that had built the *Jane Slade*. One day, Ernie Slade, Jane's grandson, asked her if she would like the figurehead of the old schooner, which was now to be broken up. Delighted, Daphne had it placed on the beam outside her bedroom window. Ernie's grandmother was buried in the churchyard at Lanteglos, he told her. Daphne visited the pretty little church on the hill above the quay at Pont and discovered the grave; then Adams brought her a box of family letters. She began to mull over a story of Janet Coombe, a free spirit driven by passionate love – of the sea, and of her son.

That October, Muriel told Daphne that if she could earn enough money to keep herself, there was no reason why she should not live at Ferryside as long as she liked. It was a huge incentive. Here was a chance for her to write the story that had been percolating in her mind, and achieve independence. That was profoundly important to her. So in the winter of 1929, she stayed across the road at The Nook, with Miss Roberts, who provided security and meals – including breakfast in bed! During the day she would go to Ferryside, to the room under the eaves at the end of the building, now identified by the figurehead from the

Jane Slade (a copy: the original is preserved inside the house) and with its windows looking down the river Fowey to the sea. There she would wrap a rug around her knees and write, losing herself in her story, which she had decided to call *The Loving Spirit* after the lines in an Emily Brontë poem: 'Alas, the countless links are strong/That bind us to our clay,/The loving spirit lingers long,/And would not pass away.'

The story would span four generations, beginning with the wedding of Janet Coombe and ending with the wedding of her great-granddaughter, Jennifer, at Lanteglos, in the churchyard of which Jennifer discovered Janet's grave 'by a thorn hedge'. (Truth can be compared to fiction, as the story of the real-life Jane Slade has been written by her great-great-granddaughter, Helen Doe.) But it is so much more than a family saga, with its portrayal of the Cornish landscape, which Daphne had come to know well and was able to convey succinctly (hedges were 'bright with hips and haws'; in the gardens 'drooped scarlet fuchsias'; in the Polmear valley 'golden bracken was waist-high and soft lichen clung to the branches of trees'), and also of nature at its stormiest.

'I can't say it's particularly enthralling at Fowey at the moment,' she wrote to Tod in January. 'It never stops raining, hailing, blowing, sleeting and snowing, so you can imagine it requires firm courage to crouch in my little hip-bath of a morning, and to creep up the garden to the outside sanitation! However, it's good for one to try and cope, and p'raps if nobody else reads the deadly book you'll spend 7/6 from kindness of heart and pretend you read the first ten pages! That is, if it's ever published at all!'

On 30 January 1930, Daphne wrote the last words of her novel and left for London. Some weeks later, she heard from Michael Joseph at Curtis Brown that Heinemann would publish her book, and she received an advance of £67 – 'a little bit of independence,' she wrote jubilantly. In the very first words of her first novel, that sense of place and the essence of Cornwall are revealed:

Janet Coombe stood on the hill above Plyn, looking down upon the harbour. Although the sun was already high in the heavens, the little town was still wrapped in an early morning mist. It clung to Plyn like a thin pale blanket, lending to the place a faint whisper of unreality as if the whole had been blessed by ghostly fingers. The tide was ebbing, the quiet waters escaped silently from the harbour and became one with the sea, unruffled and undisturbed. No straggling cloud, no hollow wind broke the calm beauty of the still white sky.

This painting of the *Jane Slade*, which was renamed the *Janet Coombe* in *The Loving Spirit*, was given to Daphne by the Slade family.

In *The Loving Spirit*, the village at the edge of the estuary where the boatyard is has become Plyn. Other landmarks of the book, so well known by Daphne from her hours of walking, can be identified in real life. The boatyard, for example, then run by the Slades and now run by the Toms family, is still there and in busy production. On an early autumn day, the still of the calm day is intermittently broken by the industrial sound of a mechanical saw as the hulk of a boat is repaired – a comforting reminder that boat-building continues and the relationship with the sea remains. On a guided walk of Fowey – one of the many organized by the Daphne du Maurier Literary Centre – one can trace the links between the book and real life. For example, 43 The Esplanade was the home of Thomas Slade, master of the *Jane Slade*, who was

View of the Fowey estuary and the village of Polruan from the hill above Pont Pill.

married twice and moved to Holly House in Polruan. The death of his second wife affected him so badly that he ended his days in the private wing of Bodmin Asylum. The parallels between him and Joseph Coombe in *The Loving Spirit*, who lived in Ivy House in Plyn, are exact.

By the time *The Loving Spirit* was published in 1932, Daphne had written another book and was halfway through a third. A trip to Paris to see Ferdy had inspired *I'll Never Be Young Again*, which took her two months, and she was working in Fowey on *The Progress of Julius* (the character of whom bore significant resemblance to her father). She was spending more and more time down there, writing to Tod in July 1931, 'I've been in Fowey since March! Yes by Jove, and don't intend returning for a long while. If I can afford it I want to make this permanent headquarters. I do feel so well and happy down here, so why not? What with boating, gardening, walking, writing, my time is full.'

She was enjoying looking after the house, not for the innate satisfaction of it but for the recognition of being successfully in charge herself. She announced that she and the cook were managing on just under £2 per week, though she added later that Muriel paid half the coal bill. But she wrote proudly that she was doing her own housekeeping:

> I sally forth with a basket on my arm and choose '4 lbs of rolled ribs of beef' and 'what are your peas today, Miss King?'! and there's the laundry 'I think we can make the sheets do another week, Mrs Staton' and then the gardener: 'Please miss, we shall want some more logs in'! It's all great fun – the sheer selfish joy of living alone and being dependent on no one.

Little by little she was achieving total independence: 'I'm happier than I've ever been in my life.' It was as though this privileged offshoot of the theatrical aristocracy had found her true *métier* at last. She was working steadily, and also revelling in small town life – she joined the Bodinnick Women's Institute, so there was a lot of 'Jerusalem, tea and buns. And if you peeped through the window you would see me scrambling round the room with all the fat farm women playing musical chairs!! Next week there is an appalling thing called a "social" . . .' She even 'tramped the countryside with poppies' in November for Remembrance Day, though it was

'pouring with rain and pitch dark'. Even the miseries of being cold and eating a 'frugal supper – fried eggs and chips' could not deflect her satisfaction, though she gratefully appreciated the cosy slippers Tod sent, ideal for when she came in 'wet and cold from hunting driftwood'.

Cornwall was proving conducive to creativity and to companionship. One important friendship was with Foy Quiller-Couch, the daughter of Arthur Quiller-Couch, who was the *eminence grise* of Fowey (as well as Mayor, Commodore of the Yacht Club and Justice of the Peace) and who became something of a mentor to her. She would often go to tea at The Haven, his house on the Esplanade with a view across his beloved estuary. Or they might go to tea at the Fowey Hotel, the rather grand building across the road. She had read Q's book *On the Art of Writing* after she had been introduced to him in Cambridge. Her acquaintance with Q led to her friendship with the historian A.L. Rowse, who had been born in Cornwall, and whom Q had encouraged to go to Oxford, thus launching him on his career as a prolific academic: when he wrote a memoir of Q in 1988 Rowse dedicated it to Daphne 'in common admiration for our old mentor and friend'. However, there were some tricky patches in Daphne's relationship with Q. Daphne's second book, *I'll Never Be Young Again*, which was about a young man and woman living together in Paris, had shocked him. She told A.L. Rowse of his summoning her to his presence, and how she sat trembling on the edge of her chair:

> He carpeted her at The Haven: 'My dear Daphne, people don't say such things,' the old innocent reproved her. The young lady, who knew, replied 'But, Sir Arthur, they *do*.' The dear old boy couldn't face the thought, especially with his old-fashioned gallantry about women, and wondered whether this made her suitable company for daughter Foy and her friend Lady Vyvyan of Trelowarren.

It seems that Q relented, as not long afterwards Daphne went on a riding expedition with Foy. They made a trip to the Lizard, the southernmost point of Cornwall, the bright waves dashing against the fearsome rocks, and to Trelowarren to meet Clara, wife of the much older Sir Courtenay Vyvyan. Daphne never forgot that visit to Trelowarren. She wrote much later, four decades on, in a preface to Clara Vyvyan's *Letters from a Cornish Garden*: 'Naïve and brash at twenty three, a newcomer to Cornwall, it was my good fortune to be befriended by Q's daughter, who took me on a riding-tour to the Helford district and beyond. I was mounted on a cob named Tom who invariably dived into the nearest hedge at the approach of traffic.' There were other problems, such as sleeting rain and saddle-soreness (she had only ridden before on a sandy track on Hampstead Heath). But they managed to reach the Lizard, staying overnight there, with the Lizard foghorn keeping her awake, as did the lighthouse beam that flashed every few seconds into her window. Then Foy took her to Trelowarren.

Daphne, already struck by the avenue of holm oaks with intertwining branches, was overwhelmed by her first sight of the eighteenth-century Gothic-style house, which came as 'a shock of surprise and delight'. It was 'the most beautiful place imaginable,' she wrote in her diary. 'I just can't believe it is true.' Her stay there remained a vivid memory; perhaps it was even a crucially formative experience. 'Few places have made such a profound impression on me,' she wrote. 'I simply hated leaving Trelowarren.'

She recalled some of her favourite moments – Clara cutting flowers in the Lady's Garden, a robin flying on to Sir Courtenay's hand, and Sir Courtenay showing her portraits of his ancestors.

Daphne was captivated by 'that ilex avenue, where the branches intertwine' at Trelowarren when she first visited Lady Clara Vyvyan, friend of Foy Quiller-Couch.

The view south from Menabilly, used on Daphne's 1952 Christmas card.

And it was during these early years in Fowey at Ferryside that she came across, for the first time, a house that was to be more significant to her than any other in her lifetime. In an essay written in 1946, 'The House of Secrets', she said that she had found in a guidebook a reference to nearby Menabilly and the fact that it had been lived in by the same family for four centuries (perhaps the guidebook was the one dated 1914, which described Menabilly as 'a domain – mostly woods – of singular beauty and richness' and instructed that 'permission to traverse them must be applied for in writing'). But elsewhere she wrote that she had seen from Gribbin Head, with its red and white-banded Daymark, the glimpse of a roof deep in the 'enchanted woods' there, and had learnt more about Menabilly from Q. Whichever it was, she and Angela were inspired to set off on a late October afternoon in 1928, with Daphne's dog Bingo and Angela's Pekingese, to try to find Menabilly, the mansion that lay to the south-west of Fowey behind handsome wrought-iron gates, which the Rashleighs had lived in for four centuries but was now unlived in and unloved. They went to Four Turnings, the crossroads above Fowey, where the beginnings of that drive can be seen beside the old east lodge. The gates – a gift from Trinity House to William Rashleigh 'in consideration of favours and concessions relative to the material and site' of the Gribbin Head Daymark – are no longer there. Neither is Tristan's stone, the monolith that once marked the burial place of King Mark's son at Castle Dore in nearby Lostwithiel, and which was, at this time, by the entrance to Menabilly; it has been moved again along the approach road to Fowey.

But it was the house itself that seems to have left the deepest mark on her: the dining room, the library filled with books, the chapel over which Sir Courtenay hoisted a St George's flag on its flagstaff, 'a stable-clock that struck the hours, then silence again, a silence centuries old'. At the end of her visit she wrote: 'This is the last of England as I will ever know it, and I wanted to weep, and hide in the walls.' Her reaction was an early indication of the impact that houses had on her, and of the profound relationship she developed with them.

Daphne and Angela determined to penetrate the 'almost Sleeping-Beauty-like legend of undergrowth which kept at bay most trespassers and sightseers', as Angela put it. It was easy enough to enter the estate, but Menabilly itself remained elusive. The sisters were soon lost in a 'veritable jungle of tropical trees, shrubs and "bush"'. Angela described the 'eerie and most ghost-like atmosphere' as they

threshed backwards and forwards, this way and that, falling into holes and over submerged tree-trunks, realising only too well that we knew neither the way to the great house nor yet the way back to Fowey. Owls by now were hooting, and strange night birds emitted shrieks and cries, the unmistakable smell of fox was frequently apparent and the dogs kept at our heels, tails down, all enjoyment vanished.

The local legend was that Menabilly was haunted, and Angela by this stage was quite convinced this was true. Eventually, as the moon came up, they found themselves near a cove they knew, at Polridmouth (pronounced 'Pridmouth'), miles from Ferryside, and Angela at least was glad to be done with the adventure.

Not so Daphne, who the next day persuaded Angela to join her in another expedition. This time they went via the west lodge, on the road past the turn-off to Polkerris. Angela was less impressed: she still remembered many years later feeling frightened by the house. 'It seemed so lonely, so gloomy, so – yes – haunted.' The sisters pressed their faces against the window panes, 'gazed at Victorian furniture . . . pictures hanging . . . a rocking horse . . . but all was sombre, and one knew that the rocking-horse had known no child for many a year, and that the house was mourning her past glory'. This grey stone manor had been one of the great houses of Cornwall and carriages had driven along the now-impassable drive where they had been lost the night before. It was hard to believe that now.

But it had captivated Daphne, as had this part of Cornwall entirely. 'The place has taken hold of me,' she wrote in her diary, as she left for London soon afterwards. 'Ships anchored, looming up through blackness. The jetties, white with clay. Mysterious shrouded trees, owls hooting, the splash of muffled oars in lumpy water, Menabilly . . . All I want is to be at Fowey. Nothing and no-one else. This, now, is my life.'

As soon as she was back the following spring she did something most uncharacteristic for someone who loved her sleep: she rose at 5.00 a.m. to visit Menabilly. Soon she was returning often, picnicking among the flaming rhododendrons, prowling round the perimeter, past the heavily carved oak door and the shuttered windows, and marvelling at the ivy that covered the facade, so much ivy that it almost seemed part of the trees. She fantasized about living there, spying inside, once climbing in through an unlatched window and wandering through the dusty abandoned rooms. A photograph taken then of the ivy-smothered mansion has her handwritten note on the back: 'Menabilly – during trespassing days 1929–30.'

She was not the only one who trespassed: A.L. Rowse wrote of visiting there one evening in 1939, while walking by the sea by the Gribbin, 'along the cliff path close to the water with drifts of bluebell and pink campion below' and then up into the grounds of Menabilly along deserted avenues and walks lined with holly, eucalyptus and ferns. 'We walked up between banks of rhododendrons to peer into the windows of the deserted house, the family portraits up in the dining-room, the big fireplaces, firedogs, Sheraton chairs, china, the confusion of the library, no-one there, the cupola falling in.'

Daphne enjoyed the lawlessness of trespassing, although in the end she wrote to the owner to ask for permission to walk in the grounds, and this was granted. Part of the mystique, the attraction, was the continuity: until now only one family had lived within its walls. Or 'her' walls, for that is how Daphne thought of Menabilly: 'One family had given her life. They had been born here, they had loved, they had quarrelled, they had suffered, they had died. And out of these emotions she had woven a personality for herself, she had become what their thoughts and desires had made her.'

The first member of the family to settle in this part of Cornwall was Philip Rashleigh, who began trading in Fowey in 1529. This was the start of a rivalry with the Treffrys, who had already been there for 200 years: their grand house, Place, is a castellated mansion tucked away in the heart of Fowey close to the church of St Fimbarrus (which is full of plaques and monuments to the two families). Rashleigh managed to establish himself, landwise, by buying some of Tywardreath Priory after the Dissolution, and another chunk of monastic land on the Gribbin peninsula. His son John carried on in his father's footsteps, buying up land that included most of what had been Bodmin Priory, and in 1555 the manor house of Thomas Healey in Market Street in Fowey, along with a cellar full of fine wines, for £6 13s. 4d. John was doing well for himself, and preferred to live in Fowey, building a house by the town quay, now the Ship Inn, in 1570: the date – along with the names 'John and Ales [Alice] Rashleigh' – is carved into the elaborate chimneypiece in the finely panelled room, then the parlour and now the main bedroom. It was his son, also John, who began to build Menabilly on the Gribbin, a task completed by the next generation: Jonathan Rashleigh saw the completion of the house in the early seventeenth century – and its sacking during the Civil War. Menabilly was entirely rebuilt in the eighteenth century, and another wing added in Victorian times. But when Daphne first saw it, it had been uninhabited for several years, as the current owner, Dr Rashleigh, lived in Devon: his wife did not care for the house, and he preferred to remain there.

Daphne, however, did care for the house, even if no one else did. Indeed, discovering Menabilly was the beginning of a love affair for her. She appears to have expressed her feelings about it in a story called 'Happy Valley', published in 1932 in the Christmas issue of the *Illustrated London News*. Happy Valley is the name later given to part of the estate of Manderley, and, as if a harbinger of the famous opening line of *Rebecca*, the story begins: 'When she first used to see the valley in dreams . . .' Those dreams had tall beech trees, a path that was tangled and overgrown, with rhododendron and hydrangea 'stretching tentacles across the pathway to imprison her', as well as a house that seemed 'part of her life, bound up in her'. In the story, the narrator is told off for day-dreaming, or 'mooning' – first by a critical aunt, and then, affectionately, by her lover – just as Daphne often was. 'Her dreaming mind, lost to the world and intensely alive in its own dream planet, would quieten and relax, would murmur in solitude, "I'm here, I'm happy, I'm home again".'

By the time she wrote this, Daphne's life had taken an unexpected turn. In the late summer of 1931 Daphne had been at Ferryside when her sister Angela spotted a rather good-looking man in a boat travelling up-river and pointed him out to Daphne. That might have been that, but it was not a chance visit: Major Browning, a much-decorated officer of the Grenadier Guards, had come to Fowey precisely because of Daphne. He had read her first book, *The Loving Spirit*, and was so taken with it that he had had an urge to visit the setting of the book, and perhaps meet its author. He had come with his close friend from the Grenadiers, John Prescott, who was a West Countryman and had aunts conveniently located en route. They had come from the Isle of Wight in Browning's boat *Ygdrasil*, named after the ash tree of Norse mythology under which the gods held daily council. Browning returned more than once that autumn with George Richards, his soldier-servant (as a batman was known in the Brigade of Guards), as crew, before laying up his boat in Hunkin's boatyard for the winter.

In April 1932, Daphne was in Fowey again, convalescing after an operation for appendicitis. So was Major Browning, who, on

Daphne and Tommy (as she called her husband, Major Frederick Browning) in his cruiser, *Ygdrasil*.

that day in each other's company but the following two as well. Browning had to return to his battalion in London, but he was back at Fowey within a week.

Daphne wrote ecstatically to Tod: 'I am brown as a berry all over from sunbathing. And what is more I am in love!!! But hush, not a word to anyone. He is the best-looking thing I have ever seen. The only snag is that he is a Major in the Grenadier Guards and I can't see myself following the Drum, can you?' But she was undaunted by that. He was smitten too. Every time he could 'he leaps down here in his car and we spend long days out at sea in his boat. We spend most of the time cursing each other for spoiling the paint on the boat and yelling warnings if a lobster pot floats near the propeller. No sighs and gazing at the moon for me, thank you.'

They made up their minds about each other within weeks. He proposed to her but she rejected him, as she didn't believe in marriage; but his friends persuaded her that his career would be wrecked if they lived together without marrying, so she then proposed to him. 'I am being married down here this month,' she announced to Tod in July. 'Cap over the mills and bridges burnt.'

hearing about her illness, wrote her a note inviting her out in his boat. Luckily for the etiquette of the time, he had discovered in the meantime that his father had met hers at the Garrick Club, so all was entirely proper.

Major Browning (christened Frederick, nicknamed 'Boy' during the First World War, but called Tommy by his family and by Daphne) was ten years older than her, but that did not prevent them getting on with each other immediately. They shared a love of the sea – and a similar sense of humour. They spent not just

CHAPTER 3
LOVE AND LANDSCAPE:
FRENCHMAN'S CREEK AND JAMAICA INN

On 19 July 1932, just three months after the couple had met, two boats left Bodinnick at 8.15 a.m. to catch the tide. One, *Cora Ann*, was carrying Daphne, her parents and her cousin Geoffrey. The other, *Ygdrasil*, was carrying Tommy and George Hunkin, who was to be best man. Their destination was St Wyllow's, the slate-roofed church at Lanteglos: the church where Daphne had found the gravestone of Jane Slade, and where Janet Coombe had married her cousin Thomas in *The Loving Spirit*, the book that had brought Tommy to Fowey in the first place. Real life was following fiction.

It was as far removed from a theatreland wedding as could be imagined. Gerald, who had burst into tears when he'd heard Daphne was to be married, saying 'It isn't fair', had cheered up with the thought of his brave soldier son-in-law, and Muriel was reconciled to the loss of a day in the limelight. There were no guests – even Angela and Jeanne were absent, as Angela was on holiday in Italy and Jeanne in Wales. There was no wedding dress; Daphne was wearing a faded blue coat and skirt, which her mother had carefully ironed. ('Daphne looked very sweet in her blue serge which I pressed the evening before,' Muriel said in a letter to Angela.) There was no reception; the wedding breakfast consisted of sausages and bacon cooked in the galley of *Ygdrasil*. There was, however, a bit of a turnout when they arrived back in the harbour: Daphne was well known and news had got out, so her neighbours were waving from houses and cottages. The Quiller-Couches rowed out to *Ygdrasil* in Q's bright red rowing boat to give Daphne and Tommy a bottle of their home-brewed sloe gin. Then the couple set sail for Frenchman's Creek.

'We couldn't have chosen anything more beautiful,' wrote Daphne. Frenchman's Creek is a tributary of the Helford River and a sublime oasis of peace and quiet. Perhaps Daphne already knew it, as Clara Vyvyan lived close by, and loved it. Or perhaps she knew it through Q, who had written a short story, 'Frenchman's Creek', describing how 'it runs up between overhanging woods from the western shore of Helford River, which flows down through an earthly paradise and meets the sea . . . where the oaks dip their branches in the high tides, where the stars are glassed all night long without a ripple, and where you may spend whole days with no company but herons and sandpipers'.

A portrait of Daphne by society photographer Compton Collier in 1932, the year of her marriage.

En route there was a moment of grief, as Daphne recounted years later, when Moppet, the dish mop Tommy had had as long as he'd had *Ygdrasil*, fell overboard, but harmony was restored. With Tommy's soldier-servant Richards conveniently on hand to buy supplies and row them out to *Ygdrasil*, a week of tranquillity ensued.

Daphne recreated sensations of that time a decade later for her novel *Frenchman's Creek*, published in 1941. She asked Q for permission to use the title, which he granted, saying he looked forward to seeing what she made of it. What she made of it was the one novel that she conceded was a romance (she fought all her life against being pigeonholed as a romantic novelist), a dashing tale of love and adventure. Dona St Columb, the spirited heroine who left London in disgust (not unlike Daphne) for her husband's Cornish mansion of Navron (echoes of Menabilly) and there met the cultured and artistic Jean-Benoit Aubery, skipper of *La Mouette* and pirate, describes her first impressions: 'Suddenly, before her for the first time, was the creek, still and soundless, shrouded by the trees, hidden from the eyes of men. She stared at it in wonder, for she had had no knowledge of its existence, this stealthy branch of the parent river creeping into her own property,

so sheltered, so concealed by the woods themselves.'

Much of the impact of *Frenchman's Creek* derives from the characterization of landscape, which is a particular strength of Daphne's writing. Even before Dona's first sight of the inlet, the spell is cast in the evocative first chapter, as Daphne describes its effect on a solitary yachtsman who goes exploring up-river in his dinghy on a night in midsummer. He pauses, resting on his paddles, aware suddenly of the deep silence of the creek, of its narrow twisting channel, and he feels 'that he is an interloper, a trespasser in time'. The passage continues:

OPPOSITE The church and churchyard of St Wyllow's at Lanteglos, burial place of Jane Slade.
ABOVE The interior of St Wyllow's, where Daphne and Tommy were married in 1932.

The trees still crowd thick and darkly to the water's edge, and the moss is succulent and green upon the little quay where Dona built her fire and looked across the flames and laughed at her lover, but today no ship lies at anchor in the pool, with rakish masts pointing to the skies, there is no rattle of chain through the hawse hole, no rich tobacco smell upon the air, no echo of voices coming across the water in a lilting foreign tongue.

Back at his yacht, the yachtsman looks back for the last time to see 'the full moon white and shining in all its summer glory rise above the tall trees . . . A night-jar churrs from the bracken on the hills, a fish breaks the surface of the water with a little plopping sound, and slowly his ship turns to meet the incoming tide, and the creek is hidden from him.'

Frenchman's Creek today retains that sense of remoteness. The waters seem utterly still, unless it has been raining all night, when the stream feeding it runs muddily, brownly, down towards the tide coming up the estuary. At low tide, the weed-covered angular skeletons of fallen trees are uncovered; abandoned boats are beached, mossy and forlorn; egrets peck in the swathes of mud at water's edge. Lapwings call, while rooks, in their communal living quarters at the top of an oak tree, vie noisily with them.

Clara Vyvyan, whose home Trelowarren had made such an impression on Daphne, frequently visited the creek and wrote lyrically about it in her book on the Helford River: 'At low tide, the Pill is only a narrow trickle of water moving down through a silent world of mud, but you could hardly imagine a more beautiful journey than rowing up its whole length on a rising and nearly full tide. As your waterway becomes narrow and narrower the trees on either shore seem to enfold you, almost as if with a personal caress.'

Tucked away among those trees is a cottage, now belonging to the Landmark Trust but for a while during the 1930s rented by Clara Vyvyan and her friend Maria Pendragon. The day they first saw it they heard cuckoos calling to each other, so they called it Cuckoo Cottage. With all the glee of small children playing house, they collected sticks in the woods about to make fires, distempered the walls in bright yellow, installed a dresser and displayed willow-pattern plates, and determined to keep it 'homely and cottagey'. They furnished it sparingly and idiosyncratically. Clara wrote of the 'gnomish stools', the bright rugs scattered round the floor and the hip baths – two hip baths, not for convivial bathing but for sitting in. She described how, draped about with chintz and stuffed with cushions at the base and at the back, the baths became their armchairs, in which they sat with their feet hanging over the edge. This could, of course, be awkward for visitors: they wanted to invite a kind neighbour, but she was of the sort of girth that made them fearful that if she sat in a hip bath, she might never be able to leave it. Fortunately, they had one 'gaffer's' chair – upright and wooden, and suitable for such a personage.

There were parties and picnics, spread out on the strip of grass by the creek, one ending in 'bowls of cream and strawberries and raspberries' that 'went round and round in a circle'. But the most evocative description was of visits in winter, when Clara would go down there alone, 'kindle a fire, settle myself in a hip-bath with a book or two beside me and enjoy complete solitude. Often, instead of reading, I would sit gazing out of the window at that wall of trees rising to the sky and feeling the quiet of the place as if it were soft music.'

That tranquillity, still so evident today, took root in Daphne's mind. Her idyllic memories from her honeymoon, recreated in her novel, show how landscape informed her creativity – but not only through lyrical description of the countryside. Fowey, for example, which also features vividly in the novel, is the setting for the audacious raid on the laden Rashleigh boat anchored in Fowey harbour. Dressed as a cabin boy, Dona has joined the pirate ship: her crucial role is to land and to call on Philip Rashleigh

Frenchman's Creek, the tributary of the Helford River where Daphne and Tommy spent their honeymoon.

with an urgent message to board his ship immediately. Her pirate lover gives directions to the Rashleigh house 'hard by the church, facing the quay', just as it is today. The Rashleigh town house would feature again in *The King's General*: now the Ship Inn, it still has a sense of those days with its higgledy-piggledy roof line and some of those mullioned windows that Dona had tremblingly secreted herself beneath.

Her mission fulfilled, Dona is forced into even more perilous endeavour by running over the rocks in wind and rain by the river to the harbour's mouth to warn the pirate ship of the impending attack on them from St Catherine's Castle – something she achieves

triumphantly despite the ill-fitting shoes she has borrowed. When the excitement is over and they are returning to Frenchman's Creek, Dona sleeps, but before she slept she thought of

Rough Tor on Bodmin Moor, which was the setting for the climax of *Jamaica Inn*.

a Dona of the future, of ten years away, to whom all this will be a thing to cherish, a thing to remember. Much will be forgotten then, perhaps, the sounds of the tide on the mud flats, the dark sky, the dark water, the shiver of the trees behind us and the shadows they cast before them, and the smell of the young bracken and the moss. Even the things we said will be forgotten, the touch of hands, the

warmth, the loveliness, but never the peace that we have given to each other, never the stillness and the silence.

As Sheila Hodges, Daphne's editor of thirty years, later pointed out, *Frenchman's Creek* reveals many aspects of what Daphne herself felt: her longing to be a boy, her desire for freedom and especially her empathy with the Cornish coast and countryside, which endured all her life. One of her last books, *Vanishing*

Cornwall, was devoted entirely to the landscape, the history and the spirit of her adopted county.

Daphne did not draw on the serene memories of her honeymoon until the turbulent days of the Second World War. Following her second and third books, *I'll Never Be Young Again* and *Julius* (as it was later retitled), quickly written and published the year after her marriage, she wrote her fourth novel, *Jamaica Inn*, which displays the strong sense of place that suffuses all her Cornish novels. *Jamaica Inn* too begins with the Helford River, near which was the tranquil home of Mary Yellan, the heroine. But after the death of her mother, she left 'the shining Helford waters' to join her aunt Patience, whose husband Joss is the landlord of Jamaica Inn, and arrives in a viscerally contrasting world in the wilds of Bodmin Moor:

> On either side of the road the country stretched interminably into space . . . mile upon mile of bleak moorland, dark and untraversed, rolling like a desert land to some unseen horizon. No human being could live in this wasted country, thought Mary, and remain like other people; the very children would be born twisted, like the blackened shrubs of broom, bent by the force of a wind that never ceased, blow as it would from east and west from north and south. Their mind would be twisted, too, their thoughts evil, dwelling as they must amidst marsh and granite, harsh heather and crumbling stone.

The violence of the landscape, set against the 'peace and quiet of Helford . . . beside the running water', is also highlighted later by the contrast with an initially carefree visit Mary makes with Joss's brother Jem to Launceston before Christmas: 'The town was set on the bosom of a hill, with a castle framed in the centre, like a tale from old history. There were trees clustered here, and sloping fields, and water framed in the valley below.' The cobbled streets and 'warmth and light of the hospitable White Hart' (still there) in Launceston are in complete opposition to the friendless atmosphere of her uncle's hostelry.

The description of Bodmin Moor as Mary first arrives there can still hold true today – especially if it is in the swirling grip of one of the frequent fogs that can suddenly descend – though the shock of Jamaica Inn today, the moor's 'one grim landmark' for Mary, dominating a ridge above the A30 at Bolventor, lies more in its touristification. This was something which Daphne felt regret about, as her book was the cause of it. She wrote in *Vanishing Cornwall*: 'As a motorist I pass by with some embarrassment, feeling myself to blame, for out of that November evening long ago came a novel which proved popular, passing, as fiction does, into the folklore of the district. As the author I am flattered, but as a one-time wanderer dismayed.'

Daphne had first visited Jamaica Inn in November 1930 on another riding expedition with Foy Quiller-Couch to Bodmin Moor. It was, she said, a place that would grip her imagination almost as much as Menabilly. Though it was then the Jamaica Inn Temperance Hotel – the influence of Methodism had transformed it in 1880, and so it remained until the Second World War – it had been a stop for stage and mail coaches travelling from Penzance or Falmouth to London, and it was not hard for Daphne to imagine scenes from that more turbulent past, when smuggling was rife.

Daphne and Foy had arrived at Jamica Inn at lunchtime, after spending the night at the Royal Hotel in Bodmin and, as Daphne told Hugh Scully on BBC's *Woman's Hour* in 1975, she wrote in her diary: 'I want to spend days here.' (Scully observed that 'places have an enormous impact on you,' and she replied, 'Oh, terrific! Absolutely terrific.') Later that day, Daphne and Foy set out on horseback across the moor to visit 'old Lady Rodd' at Trebartha Hall, but were quickly lost. The moor was 'desolate, sinister'. In one of those sudden changes of weather to which Bodmin Moor is prone, the sky blackened and rain cascaded down. They sheltered in the ruins of a cottage until the rain had ceased, to be replaced by thick fog. 'There's nothing for it but to get into the saddle, leave our reins loose on their necks and let them lead us home,' said Foy, an experienced horsewoman. The anxious period following, in the dark, 'on, forever on, nothing on all sides but waste and moor', was suddenly ended when they came across 'the blessed streaky wetness of the Launceston–Bodmin road and surprisingly, unbelievably, the gaunt chimneys of Jamaica Inn itself'. As her diary recorded, 'we sat wearily to our supper and I was immeasurably happy.' 'In an instant 'fear was forgotten, danger had never been . . . here was the turf fire for which we had longed, brown and smoky sweet, a supper of eggs and bacon ready to be served with a pot of scalding tea.' The fear was gone, the danger had never been, but the memory of that fear and the dramatic potential of that memory – which was reinforced by a later visit, when she sat by the peat fire reading *Treasure Island* (and had a chance meeting with a vicar there) – remained with her until she wrote *Jamaica Inn*.

Daphne felt obliged to add a disclaimer at the start of her novel: 'Jamaica Inn stands today, hospitable and kindly, a temperance house on the twenty-mile road between Bodmin and Launceston. In the following story of adventure I have pictured it as it might have been over a hundred and twenty years ago; and although existing place-names figure in these pages, the character and events described are entirely imaginary.'

The rattling good yarn of smugglers and wrecking, published in 1936, was an instant best-seller. Alfred Hitchcock made it into a film, though Hollywood convention demanded that the villainous role of the Vicar of Altarnun be altered, and Charles Laughton, as the producer as well as the star, hammed it up in the newly invented role of Sir Humphrey Pengallan, a wicked squire.

Jamaica Inn has made the most of its celebrity, with bedrooms named after Joss, Jem and Patience, a brass plate set into flagstones in the bar inscribed 'Joss Merlyn was murdered here',

and performances of the novel staged in the courtyard. (And in a surprising piece of PR, the one link given on the National Portrait Gallery website's display of portraits of Daphne is to the website of Jamaica Inn, with its cunningly creaking inn sign.) The inn has paid due respect to the author responsible for its fame. In 1990, the Daphne du Maurier Memorial Room was opened, with a careful selection of objects associated with her, from a writing desk and chairs from her home at Kilmarth, photographs, a box of du Maurier cigarettes, a suitcase with her initials and a mass of photographs and newspaper cuttings and books inscribed by Daphne 'for Jamaica Inn' as well as foreign editions of her novels: *Rebecca* in Hebrew, *Frenchman's Creek* in Rumanian, *The House on the Strand* in Icelandic.

Jamaica Inn also has what must be the biggest gift shop ever attached to a pub (and coach parks to cater for the customers from Germany, Australia and America). This started off as a couple of shelves near the bar before graduating to a room in the inn. In those days, another best-selling author, Alastair Maclean, owned Jamaica Inn. He owned it for a decade but only stayed once – and he never allowed his books to be sold there. After moving out into the stable block, the shop was transferred into its own building, and then doubled in size to become the emporium that it is today, selling among other things Jamaica Inn T-shirts, beer mugs and fridge magnets, as well as a big display of Daphne's books.

But one can easily recapture the menacing sense of mystery and suspense by deviating away from the hospitable blaze of the inn on to the barren moor. Nearby is Dozmary Pool, a painting of which gripped Mary when she saw it at the Altarnun vicarage.

Jamaica Inn was published in 1936 and became an instant best-seller. Alfred Hitchcock's film of the book, which Daphne heartily disliked, was released in 1939.

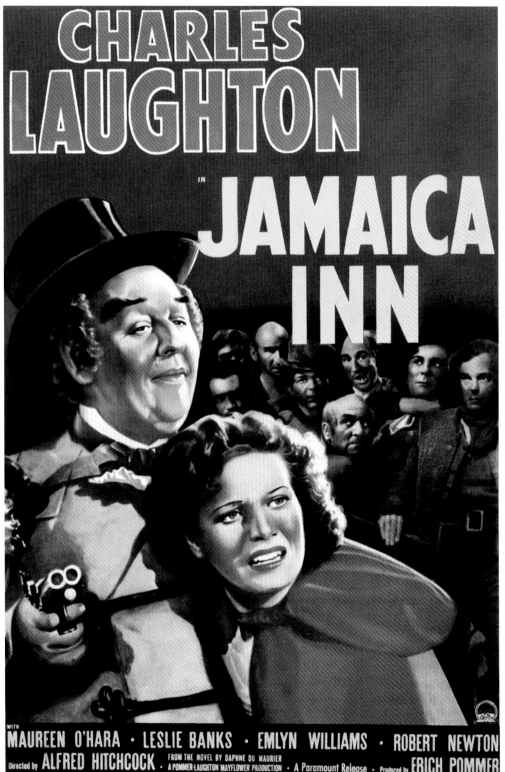

Jamaica Inn
Daphne du Maurier

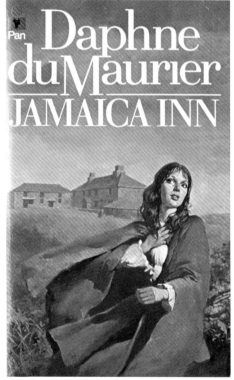

ABOVE The pub sign erected in 1990 at Jamaica Inn at Bolventor replaced an image of a highwayman with a pirate and shipwreck inspired by Daphne's novel.

OPPOSITE The church of St Nonna in Altarnun, whose vicar, Francis Davey, Mary Yellan met on Bodmin Moor in *Jamaica Inn*.

The bottomless lake of legend, into which the sword Excalibur was thrown after King Arthur was slain, can, as Daphne describes in *Vanishing Cornwall*, be still and limpid on a bright day but 'once a whisper of a breeze ripples its surface' quickly becomes a desolate and uneasy place.

Daphne seems to have known the moor well in all its moods, from the highest tor, Brown Willy (its bathetic name belies its Cornish origins, Bron Wennyly meaning 'hill of swallows'), 'lifting its head in lonely splendour', to Altarnun (Cornish for 'afternoon'), a few miles to the east, which she saw on her second visit to Jamaica Inn.

With its stream spanned by a fifteenth-century packhorse bridge and the imposing church of St Nonna, justifiably dubbed Cathedral of the Moors, Altarnun is a pretty village, rather at odds with the sinister connections in *Jamaica Inn*. The Georgian-style rectory where the infamous vicar lived is now a private house, Penhallow Manor, but it is recognizable from Daphne's description.

In February 1935, Daphne had signed a contract to write a novel for her new publisher, Victor Gollancz, and she had begun to make notes about the inn that had so fired her imagination. Later that year, she and Tommy broke their usual trip to Fowey at Bodmin Moor, staying 'miles from the nearest town, and not a sound except curlews and skylarks'; it was 'too lovely'. That did not deflect her in the slightest from her bleak depiction of the moor and the evil goings-on there, which she completed that autumn.

Jamaica Inn and *Frenchman's Creek* compellingly portray very different aspects of the landscape of Cornwall. When she finished *Jamaica Inn,* her breakthrough novel, she was staying in her beloved Fowey, at Ferryside. The next novel, the one that was to be associated with her – and with Cornwall – above all others, was to be written far away.

CHAPTER 4
MARRIAGE AND MILITARY HOMES

The first home which Daphne and Tommy lived in after their marriage was just around the corner from her parents – or, more accurately, at the bottom of their garden. It was one of the pair of Queen Anne cottages that belonged to Cannon Hall, and Gerald and Muriel turned Cannon Hall Cottage over to Daphne. The cottage was convenient, as Tommy's battalion was based in London, at Wellington Barracks in Westminster. Set back from the road on the corner of Well Road and Christchurch Hill, today it is discreetly screened by the shrubs in the front garden.

Daphne wrote to Tod – on notepaper newly embossed in scarlet (a miniature emblem, the wings from the Browning coat of arms, had been added to the address) – to clear up a misconception: 'The cottage at Hampstead was the wedding present, <u>not</u> Ferryside at all! Newspapers always muddle everything,' before adding: 'Don't you get a laugh at the thought of me being married! Every now and again it gives me quite a jerk as I look down at my ring.' Tommy was, she added, 'quite the most charming person in the world', though he did have his moods 'like all of us' and was 'a bit sorry for himself when he has a cold in the head!! (Men are all alike in that respect!)'

In 2011 the Heath and Hampstead Society mounted a plaque noting Daphne's residence from 1932 to 1934. It was unveiled by Daphne's elder daughter, Tessa, now Lady Montgomery, who was born there on 15 July 1933 – the same year Daphne's second and third books were published. 'All that fuss and sweat resulting from a moment's flash in the pan, so to speak, grossly overrated as a form of amusement,' Daphne wrote wryly to Tod. She had already chosen the name Christian (from Christian in *The Pilgrim's Progress*, with whom she had wholly identified when she was small), so the arrival of a baby girl was not in the plan. But she noted with approval that the new baby was 'well formed', and had 'strong limbs and nice skin'. Daphne was longing for sea air, writing: 'Tommy has gone to the boat for the weekend. I would have gone too but am still acting as Dairy.' She didn't want to leave Tessa at 'so tender an age'. But soon Daphne and family were on their way to Fowey, and Tessa was christened at St Wyllow's in Lanteglos.

Daphne found a 'trustworthy young girl', Margaret Eglesfield, who was to stay with the family as a nanny for several years. Daphne was quite a detached mother – from time to time, Tessa would be

Tommy, pictured in 1944 when a lieutenant-general and Commander of 1st Airborne Corps. He had a distinguished army career and was knighted in 1946.

Her father had once said to her that if he were to write his own memoir, it would have to be completely truthful, and she decided that this was what she would now be. She wrote her biography, *Gerald: A Portrait*, in four months and it was published two months later by Victor Gollancz. This was the start of her life-long association with the firm. Though critics were to say, and she was to admit, that there is a great deal of herself in the characters in her fiction, she is conspicuously low-profile in this book; she makes very little reference to herself and when she does she adopts an interesting style, writing of herself in the third person. Her portrait of her father is sympathetic but realistic, bringing out his failings as well as his virtues, and her affectionate portrayal of his character is leavened with sustained passages of humour. The frankness of the book caused some ripples, as she alludes to his 'stable' of young actresses. Friends of the family thought she had gone too far: 'A lot of people were very shocked,' she said later. But for Daphne, perhaps, it acted as a form of catharsis. She remained devoted to her father throughout her life, displaying portraits and photographs of him and surrounding herself with his possessions.

On her father's death, Cannon Hall had to be sold. There was no alternative. An elaborate brochure for this 'Fascinating Freehold Old Georgian home', which was 'For many years the Home of the late Sir Gerald du Maurier' and had many 'historical associations', was produced. It must have been poignant for the family to see the beloved family rooms pictured and described for all the world to see. But selling it was the only way that Muriel would be able to survive. Fortunately for her, in order to pay some of his debts to the Inland Revenue that had dogged his last few years, Gerald had signed a sponsorship deal with a tobacco company for du Maurier cigarettes – to be packaged in elegant square packets, bright red with silver band – though he never smoked them himself. Now, after his death, the royalties would continue to be paid to his widow.

despatched with Nanny to stay with one or other grandmother or to Nanny's own home – but she was not impervious to her daughter's charms, updating Tod on her development: 'she is getting very talkative and is priceless'.

In April 1934 came a shattering blow: the unexpectedly sudden death of her father from cancer, at home on 11 April, the thirty-first anniversary of his wedding day. He was buried in the churchyard of Hampstead's parish church in Church Row, the street where he had been born. Daphne did not go to his funeral, but later she went into the local church in Frimley, where she and Tommy were then living. It was then, in the quietness, that she determined to begin his biography – she said later that as soon as Gerald died, 'I *knew* that I'd have to write his life.'

du MAURIER

FILTERED FOR FLAVOUR

THE CIGARETTE WITH THE EXCLUSIVE FILTER

OPPOSITE Muriel, outside Ferryside, with her one of her Pekingeses. She had begun keeping them in 1912.
RIGHT In 1929, Gerald, pursued by the Inland Revenue, lent his name to du Maurier cigarettes, which eased his and his family's perilous finances. They are still sold in Canada.

Muriel, with Angela and Jeanne, moved to the cottages at the bottom of the garden (Cannon Hall Cottage having reverted to Muriel after Gerald's death), converting them into one house and renaming it Providence Corner, while they spent their summers at Ferryside. Only the year before Gerald's death, in 1933, the family had come close to selling Ferryside to actor friends Bart and Edna Marshall, who had often stayed there during the holidays, but Gerald had, at the last moment, pulled out of the sale: 'I can't explain why, but I feel it would be a terrible mistake.' In 1937, the family moved to live there permanently.

Meanwhile, Daphne, as the wife of a soldier, was frequently on the move. She was, she wrote in an article called 'Moving House', never more than eighteen months in the same place. This did not greatly worry her, 'because my husband organised everything, even to writing out the labels for the removal men and deciding where the various pieces of furniture should go'.

Even with these temporary short-term homes, Daphne felt a measure of affinity for the actual house: 'I would wander round in a daze, trying to picture the sort of people who had lived in the house before.' She often felt sorry for the house she had just left – 'I was sure that it would be melancholy without us' – though that feeling soon passed, as she would 'grow' into the new house, 'taking something of its atmosphere into myself and giving something in return'.

One telling detail is that Daphne's later rigid dependence on routines – her 'routes' as she called them, in the du Maurier code that she and Tommy and then her children used – may have owed much to her husband, who would always make the new home as much like the old one as possible, 'for though very go-ahead and progressive as a soldier, he was a stickler for routine in personal life.' So all the familiar objects and ornaments would be placed in exactly the same order, and pieces of furniture would be placed in new living rooms in identical corners.

In 1934, Tommy's battalion had been posted to Aldershot, and Daphne went with him to the Old Rectory, a rather beautiful Queen Anne house, in Frimley in Surrey. There was more headed notepaper, to tell Tod about her new duties, such as visiting soldiers – including the wife of a private with nine children under nine living in one room, three of whom were not walking. This is where, the following year, she started *Jamaica Inn*, her breakthrough book: she had received an advance of £1,000 and in the first three months it sold more than her previous three books put together.

In 1936, Tommy's battalion was stationed in Alexandria. It was the beginning of a period that was both drab and extraordinarily fecund. Daphne hated Egypt. She wasn't even impressed by the Pyramids: 'Just like a couple of slack heaps, my dear, on a thing like the Great West Road. And they talk about the glamour of Egypt!' She disliked the life of a military wife there, though she did her best to live up to it. She detested the heat and the environment. 'The worst point in Alexandria is the fearful damp heat. You sit inside your house and pour with sweat, without moving.' The house, at 13 Rue Jessop, did not endear itself to her. Tessa, who celebrated her third birthday there, remembers the 'great sandy beach' on the shores of the Mediterranean, which was perhaps some compensation for Daphne, as she was a strong and regular swimmer; and there was a holiday in Cyprus, where Daphne found it 'such a joy to be amongst trees and hills again'. She dealt with her disaffection, as much as was possible, by losing herself in her work, and by delving into her family history and exploring her fascination with her antecedents from her great-great-grandparents. In 1936, she completed *The Du Mauriers*, dedicated to 'the thirty-one descendants of Louis-Mathurin Busson du Maurier'. But though her family history had often provided solace as well as inspiration for her, she had not particularly enjoyed this project.

She had the perfect excuse to return to England in January 1937, as she was expecting another child. Flavia was born on 2

Daphne with her daughters,
Tessa (right) and Flavia, outside
Ferryside.

Greyfriars, which Daphne and Tommy rented when he was stationed at Aldershot in 1937, and where Daphne completed *Rebecca*.

April. 'The child literally whizzed out. Don't really mind half so much this time about not having a boy. Third time lucky?!!' Tommy, given three months' leave in May, came over to meet his new daughter, and there was a trip back to Fowey in July, much anticipated but disappointing in the event. Because of the 'frustrations of dealing with the demands of house keeping, giving a hand with the baby, answering Tessa's questions and rushing to the boats to help Tommy', Daphne felt 'torn between too many evils!'

Later that year, she went back to Egypt with Tommy, leaving Tessa and Flavia in the care of their nanny and grandmother. In the heat she pined for her beloved Cornwall, which seemed to be becoming more of a distant dream, as she was condemned to the life of a camp follower. She followed the routine of a military

wife as dutifully as she could, but her 'longing for Fowey' was intense. It was this dislocation that led to her incubation of the novel that was forever to be associated with her, set in the house of her dreams.

She began to make notes about a young woman who, on marrying an older man, a widower, is full of insecurity and jealous of her predecessor. Daphne herself had had a predecessor in Jan

Ricardo, Tommy's former fiancée. But this new novel was as much about the widower's house, Manderley, which had been in the family for generations, and the passionate feelings aroused by this house, which was so like Menabilly. 'Last night I dreamt I went to Manderley again,' one of the most famous opening lines of any novel, leads into a description of the drive, the trees, the first view of the house – a description that could have been taken straight from her trespassing days:

> The drive wound away in front of me, twisting and turning . . . Nature had come into her own again, and little by little, in her stealthy, insidious way had encroached upon the drive with long tenacious fingers. The woods, always a menace even in the past, had triumphed in the end. They crowded, dark and uncontrolled, to the borders of the drive . . . Scattered here and again amongst this jungle growth I would recognize shrubs that had been landmarks in our time, things of culture and grace, hydrangeas whose blue heads had been famous. No hand had checked their progress and they had gone native now, rearing to monster height without a bloom, black and ugly . . .

In the dream the young woman comes upon the house as Daphne must have done that first time with Angela: 'secretive and silent as it had always been, the grey stone shining in the moonlight of my dream, the mullioned windows reflecting the green lawns and the terrace. Time could not wreck the perfect symmetry of those walls, nor the site itself, a jewel in the hollow of a hand.'

But the splendid interior of Menabilly, the great stone hall with its 'exquisite staircase leading to the minstrels' gallery', the library and the ballroom, was taken from Milton Hall, another house that had been in the same family for 400 years. Daphne had visited Milton, near Peterborough, in the autumn of 1917, when Muriel had taken her three daughters to visit Evie Fitzwilliam, a former

actress friend of hers, who lived there. Daphne remembered the mansion, set in a park of 23,000 acres with a drive of 2 miles, as being 'long grey-walled, stone, stretching endlessly, great windows set one upon the other with criss-cross window panes, then more stone, and columns, while to the left the building turned to form a sort of square, crowned by a clock-tower'.

And what had stayed with Daphne ever since was 'the magnificence of the great hall, the high ceiling, the panelled walls, and those portraits hanging upon them, men with lace collars, knee-breeches, coloured stockings, four centuries of Fitzwilliams'. The blending of that childhood experience which had 'never been surpassed for 60 years' with the magical grounds of Menabilly fused into Manderley. In her waking self, the nameless heroine of *Rebecca* determines not to be bitter; she would remember 'the murmur of the sea coming up to us from the lawns below. I would think of the blown lilac, and the Happy Valley' with its azaleas and rhododendrons, 'not blood-coloured like the giants in the drive, but salmon, white, and gold, things of beauty and grace, dropping their lovely, delicate heads in the soft summer rain'.

Caught up in the bliss of creation and memories of her 'house of secrets', Daphne filled her notebook, as was her practice, with sketched-out chapters (published decades later as *The Rebecca Notebook*). That was always the 'greatest thrill' – when she had the chapters in her notebook. Back later that year in England, where Tommy was stationed at Aldershot, they rented the home of a friend of Tommy's who had taken over from him in Alexandria: a Tudor house, partly half-timbered and with many gables, called Greyfriars. There they were reunited with their daughters: Tessa remembers a comfortable house with a large rambling garden. Daphne wrote later of being happy at Greyfriars, and of writing *Rebecca* 'sitting on the window seat of the living room, typewriter propped up on the table before me'. Greyfriars is no longer there: a housing estate is in its place.

Published in 1938, *Rebecca* was pretty much an instant

sensation, gripping the imagination of people around the world. The first print run was 20,000 copies; within a few weeks, 100,000 had been sold. Neville Chamberlain took a copy with him to Germany to distract himself on his visit to meet Hitler at Berchtesgarden. Alfred Hitchcock wanted to film it; he had read the galley proofs before making the film of *Jamaica Inn*, which had almost scuppered his plans: Daphne needed much convincing that his version of *Rebecca* would be more faithful to the spirit of the novel.

The first adaptation of *Rebecca*, however, was by Orson Welles in December 1938 for the Campbell Playhouse. This was a creditable radio production, despite being punctuated by lengthy accolades of 'those fine Campbell's soups' – even by Margaret Sullavan, the star of the drama, who in a stagey little exchange with Orson Welles announced, 'I love a good story and I love a good soup.' A particular interest of this broadcast was a brief interview 'by special short wave communication' with the author. In this a confident-sounding Daphne congratulated the cast on a 'splendid interpretation'. Margaret Sullavan asked a question which showed the tremendous impact that Daphne's 'sense of place' in her novels had had on readers: 'Your descriptions of Manderley are so vivid – America is curious to know if there is really a place on an estate like Manderley.' Daphne replied: 'The next time you come to London, get into a train at Paddington Station. After 250 miles, get out of the train and walk south east for half an hour. You will come to an iron gate, a lodge and a narrow twisting drive. If you ever find your way to the end of that drive, you *may* discover Manderley.'

Within a short time, Daphne herself – not surprisingly, with her theatrical background – had adapted *Rebecca* for the stage: she finished the play in the middle of 1939. Hitchcock's film of *Rebecca,* starring Laurence Olivier and Joan Fontaine, was released the following year. It mostly met with Daphne's approval: the plot did remain faithful to the original, apart from the change to

the way Rebecca died, an adaptation required by the Hollywood Production Code. David Selznick, the producer, sent Daphne a note expressing the 'fervent hope that we haven't let you down'.

In 1939 Tommy was made Commandant of the Small Arms School, the rather more modern name given to the School of Musketry in 1919, and at the end of August he and Daphne (for fear of invasion, the children were staying with Nanny) moved to the Commandant's House in Hythe. This was 'a quite decent house, and not a bad garden' (it was 'bursting with produce'), close to the Royal Military Canal, which had been dug to defend Kent in case of invasion by Napoleon. Though the house remains, the barracks, built around the same time, have been demolished, and the area has been given the name of Musketry Park.

While living in Hythe, Daphne received a letter from her sister Angela telling her that there was to be a sale at Menabilly. Did she want anything from there? 'Did I want anything? I wanted her, my house,' she wrote in 'The House of Secrets'. 'I wanted every stick of furniture from the Jacobean oak to the Victorian bamboo. But what was the use? The war had come.'

She couldn't get down to writing – 'it all seems so pointless at the present time' – and was irritated by getting a demand for information about her next book from America:

> I wrote a rather thick letter back, saying as the New York office was many thousands of miles away perhaps they did not realise that this country was faced with the biggest crisis in history and almost certain invasion, that I was busy writing letters for the Grenadier Relief Committee, that my husband was going abroad at any moment and that 'vast sums for the next novel' seemed a little beside

Rebecca, published in 1938, quickly became Daphne's most famous novel, selling around the world. Hitchcock's acclaimed film *Rebecca* was released in 1940.

Could the *Secret of Manderley* destroy their love?

Selznick International PRESENTS

Rebecca

starring
LAURENCE OLIVIER · JOAN FONTAINE
hero of "Wuthering Heights"   *in her sensational starring debut*
with
GEORGE SANDERS · **JUDITH ANDERSON**
Directed by **ALFRED HITCHCOCK** · *From the best-selling novel by* **DAPHNE DU MAURIER**
Produced by **DAVID O. SELZNICK** *who made "Gone With The Wind"* · Released thru **UNITED ARTISTS**

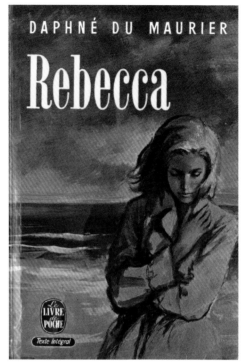

DAPHNÉ DU MAURIER

Rebecca

daphné du maurier
REBECCA

BIBLIOTHEQUE DES SUCCES

the point! The sordid commercial outlook of people still makes me quite sick.

Having barely had time to use the headed notepaper, she and Tommy were on the move again. Now a brigadier, Tommy moved with the 128th Infantry Brigade, not abroad but to Hertfordshire: he would have accommodation, of course, but Daphne was homeless. She stayed briefly in London with Tommy's sister, Grace, who had a flat in Whitelands House in the King's Road, having packed the children off to Fowey, while Johnson, Tommy's new soldier-servant, searched for a place in Hertfordshire for Daphne, with the children, to be a paying guest. He struck lucky. In July 1940, Daphne wrote to Tod that she had 'found an asylum (or rather haven) with some perfectly charming people called Puxley, who have a delightful Lutyens house'.

Langley End, 4 miles south of Hitchin, was one of a number of houses designed by Edwin Lutyens for Herbert and Violet Fenwick, who had commissioned additions to their Queen Anne mansion Temple Dinsley. Other houses were for the estate builder, estate carpenter and estate farmer; and Hill End, as it was first called, sited on the brow of a hill rising above a wooded cleft – the roof and great chimneys, a Lutyens characteristic, could be seen above the trees – had been built for Violet Fenwick (the couple divorced in 1917). The owners in 1940 were Paddy and Christopher Puxley, whom Daphne found 'most congenial. I breakfast in bed and wander the garden, and go for walks to my heart's content.'

She had brought her housemaid, who 'helps Mrs P's maids'. The children, plus Nanny and a nursery maid called Prim, arrived and were given a suite of rooms in a separate wing that looked out over the stable yard and garages. Daphne herself had her own bedroom, dressing room and modern bathroom. Tommy was able to come over to Langley End at night. Tessa and Flavia enjoyed the spacious grounds and the attention: they were affectionately

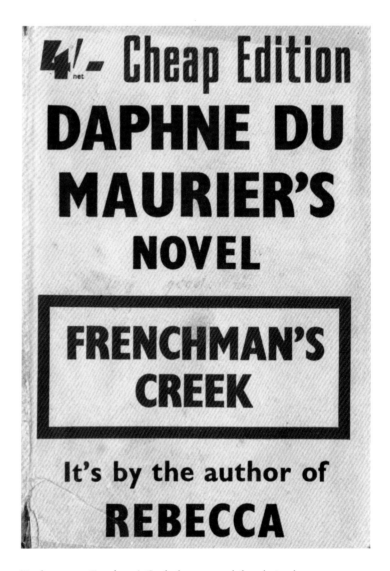

Daphne wrote *Frenchman's Creek*, the one novel she admitted was a romance, four years after *Rebecca* in 1941, nearly a decade after her honeymoon there.

tended by Paddy and Christopher, who had no children of their own. And Daphne, who had been persuaded to put together *Come Wind, Come Weather*, a 'sixpenny booklet' of stories for the Moral Re-armament Movement, with royalties going to the Soldiers' Families Association and to be published by Heinemann, was able to work.

But at summer's end, there was another move to a nearby house called Cloud's Hill, which belonged to Lord Lloyd, Secretary of State for the Colonies. The move was necessary, as Daphne was expecting another baby: 'I thought the time had come for another effort at a son but I'm quite prepared for another lumping daughter.' She was rather disgruntled that Lady Lloyd 'locked up the best china!' Still, it was a pleasant home with a large lawn ending in a ha-ha. Entertainment was provided by the neighbouring family, whose eight daughters became known as the 'Brigade Butterflies', and would sometimes gallop their horses over to the ha-ha, where Tessa and Flavia would feed the horses.

For Daphne, it was, indeed, third time lucky: 'Well, I've done it at last! For seven years I've waited to see "Mrs Browning – a son" in *The Times*!' Christian was born on 3 November, very swiftly, taking 'a violent header out of me and landed in the bed, yelling as he did so!' Flavia and Tessa could only look on with amazement as their kind but slightly distant mother hugged and kissed their new brother, even bathing him, rather than leaving such chores to Nanny.

Full of good cheer, and anticipating a wedding she was planning to attend, she wrote to Tod, who had in the 1930s set up a millinery business with a partner: 'I suppose there's no chance of your being able to make me a couple of hats. I have one of these new Baby Seal (dyed blue fox) fur coats from Fenwicks. The Fenwick hats to match are hideous.' She also longed for 'a little fur cap . . . and a jaunty rust country felt to go with my various tweeds'. Her letters to Tod were frequently peppered with requests and progress reports on Tod's hats, such as on the Panama, which had been particularly successful in Egypt; she was a loyal customer.

After Christmas, as she had feared, the Lloyds moved back to Cloud's Hill (Lord Lloyd died suddenly the following month) and she was again faced with homelessness. Though the Puxleys had now taken in some evacuees, they invited her to return to Langley End – along with '3 children, nanny, nursemaid and housemaid!

Angelic of them'. Daphne had an idea for a new book, *Frenchman's Creek*, and she was soon at work on it, relaying snippets of the story to the children.

But this stay at Langley End was not so congenial. There was a series of mishaps. Nanny became ill: a nervous collapse, brought on perhaps, Daphne thought, by having too much responsibility for the children the previous year. 'So I have had to take on Christian!' Luckily, he had 'the temperament of an angel, and smiled happily throughout my bungling management'. She was involved with Christian – soon to be called Kits by his sisters, and then by everyone – in a way that she had never been with her daughters, though because he was, from the beginning, good-natured and funny, Tessa and Flavia did not object.

Despite her contentment, Daphne found looking after Kits exhausting. She wrote to Angela that after the late feed, 'one is never in bed until eleven-thirty and then up again at six – and you know I worship sleep – I'm sure it's all very good discipline for me, so indolent by nature.'

Added to this, illness struck the family: Tessa and Flavia got measles in turn, and Daphne found herself 'rushing about with bed-pans, brewing little drinks, then mixing bottles for Christian and changing napkins, and if one has a *moment* to spare one dashes to the typewriter to scribble a page of *Frenchman's Creek*'. This was finally published in 1941, dedicated to Paddy and Christopher. Then Daphne herself collapsed, with pneumonia. She recovered slowly, lying on the sofa in the drawing room while Christopher Puxley, ever attentive, played the piano to her.

However, the greatest mishap of all was to come, when, on a spring day in 1942, Paddy walked into the room to find her husband and Daphne embracing. Life at Langley End could not be the same again. It was time to go home to Cornwall.

CHAPTER 5
THE MAGNETISM OF MENABILLY

In April 1942 Daphne moved back to Fowey. She could not live at Ferryside, as it had been requisitioned by the Royal Navy – her mother and sisters had taken a house on the Esplanade in Fowey – so she rented 8 Readymoney Cove. This was by the small bay nestling between Covington Woods – with its paths up to St Catharine's Castle in one direction and the Gribbin in the other – and Point Neptune, an imposing Victorian Italianate house of granite on the edge of the estuary. A guidebook of 1892 describes Point Neptune as 'the beautiful and pleasantly situated marine residence of William Rashleigh esquire', commending its fine view of the harbour, the carriage road leading to it that wound its way alongside the high slate wall, and the footpath at its side, 'the use of which Mr Rashleigh and his lady have generously and opportunely presented to the respectable inhabitants of Fowey of all classes'. Their new home had once been the coach house and stable block of Point Neptune (perhaps that was the cause of the abundance of black beetles there remembered by Tessa and Flavia). So Daphne's direct association with the Rashleighs began.

After the spacious comfort of Langley End, Readymoney was cramped, but it suited Daphne well: 'Just the right size for us without Tommy, as I rather "pig" it by having my meals in the sitting room and am using the servant's bathroom and a funny little upstairs bedroom,' she wrote to Tod, 'while the children swamp the remainder and have the dining room as a day nursery.' She had a cook 'and a daily minion comes in and gives a hand with housework. Margaret does the housekeeping. So I can't complain of being overworked.'

For the children, there was a large garden with lawns, shrubbery, tennis court and a stream running through it. ('Readymoney' derives from *rid* and *maen*, meaning 'stream by the rock'.) The greatest attraction, however, was the beach across the road. To prevent enemy landings, it was studded with tall iron bars, on which, as Flavia relates, the children were forbidden to climb; so there was the added illicit pleasure of slipping the noose and racing down to the beach to swing on the bars, and then rushing back to squirrel away the telltale wet clothes. The children settled into a routine; Tessa was enrolled at St David's school along the Esplanade, where Flavia in due course joined her. Daphne was glad to be back in Cornwall, though Fowey was becoming very militarized: no boats were allowed on the river, so she could not

The magnificent staircase and moulded ceiling of Menabilly. On the wall is Frederic Whiting's portrait of the three du Maurier sisters, set on Hampstead Heath.

use theirs, and Polridmouth Beach was to be closed to the public.

Daphne's links with Langley End had not ended with her departure. In July, Christopher Puxley visited her, staying at the Fowey Hotel. 'He is quite the nicest man I know (after Tommy!),' she wrote with insouciance to Tod, 'and so I was very pleased to see him again.' They spent their days at the Watch House, a little coastguard's hut across the bay. The new novel Daphne was writing was heavily influenced by Puxley: *Hungry Hill*, a passionate tale of five generations of an Irish family and of a copper mine with which their fortunes and fate were closely linked, was based heavily on the stories she had heard from him about his ancestors in their long conversations at Langley End. It was published in 1943, though it did not garner as much appreciation as her earlier books.

8 Readmoney Cove, where Daphne and her family lived from 1942 to 1943, before she gained a lease on Menabilly.

She needed a new project, but the project that she wanted most of all, now that she was back in her beloved Cornwall, was Menabilly. She had inhabited it in her mind while writing *Rebecca* seven years before, but the fiction could not satisfy the yearning she had for the actual house. What she had felt about it years before when she had trespassed still held true: 'Here was a block of stone, even as the desert Sphinx, made by man for his own purpose – yet she had a personality that was hers alone, without the touch of human hand.'

She hadn't revisited Menabilly since the war had begun. But now she made her pilgrimage, and found a house that looked, she thought, like a blitzed building: it was almost derelict. The sale Angela had told her about had largely emptied it of furniture; the windows were broken; fungus was growing on ceilings and walls. Years of neglect had wrought terrible change. 'Moisture everywhere, death and decay. I could scarcely see the soul of her for the despair,' she wrote later.

Daphne was deeply distressed. Her instinctive identification with bricks and mortar, seen so long ago at Clara Vyvyan's house,

Trelowarren, and even, to a lesser extent, at the houses she had moved through with her husband, now surfaced more strongly than ever. 'Have you seen a man who has once been handsome and strong go unshaven and unkempt? Have you seen a woman lovely in her youth raddled beneath the eyes, her hair tousled and grey? Sadder than either, more bitter and more poignant, is a lonely house.'

This return visit left her angry and determined. To see the house she loved disintegrating before her eyes seemed unbearable. She phoned her lawyer, Walter Graham, and asked him to write to Dr Rashleigh – the same Dr Rashleigh who had allowed her to walk in the grounds – to ask if he would let it to her. To her astonishment, Graham came to see her a week later, saying that Dr Rashleigh had agreed. However, Graham added, he didn't see how she could live there all the time: there was dry rot, a leaking roof, no electricity, no hot-water system. No doubt he advised her to buy another house, any house: that would have been the sensible option. The list of reasons why she should not go ahead did not, of course, deter Daphne in the slightest. Menabilly was all she wanted, and she grasped her opportunity with both hands.

She could afford it. Money was no problem, especially after the publication of *Frenchman's Creek*, though much of it was going to the Inland Revenue, as she lamented in a letter to Tod: 'With selling film rights etc, I earned last year £25,000. I thought my fortune was made. I have just heard that £22,500 is to be taken in tax.' The proceeds of her book, she calculated, had given the government enough to build a Lancaster bomber: she was seriously thinking of going about with a placard saying that she was a benefactress.

There was endless negotiation: 'Dr Rashleigh is being so frightfully grasping, and wants me to do everything and him absolutely nix. The trouble is that I so much want to go there that I'd rather be rooked than not go, and of course the old boy realises it and can ask what he likes.' Dr Rashleigh was, no doubt, fully aware of the resources of – and the market value of Menabilly to – his supplicant.

Daphne and Angela took the children to visit it for a picnic. Flavia remembers how her mother 'put her hands out and buried them in the ivy, leaning her cheek against it, kissing the house. When she came back towards us, her face was slightly flushed, her blue eyes very bright, almost dancing with some secret joy.'

In the end a deal was struck. She wrote to Tommy to tell him of her decision (his reaction, she said, was to tell his brother officers 'I am afraid Daphne has gone mad', but he was far away, in Tunis, and immersed in war); then she set about working out the finances and applying for grants. She was quite astute about money, having from the beginning of her housekeeping days at Ferryside kept notes of her accounts, and had put much of her income into trusts – as A.L. Rowse acknowledged rather enviously ('Shrewd old Walter Graham of Fowey had done better for her in time than the grandest London lawyers.'). She managed to obtain £250 from the newly formed Ministry of Works, which was enough to pay for a large portion of the renovation required, and in August she wrote to Tod that the 'Menabilly plan is going ahead at last.' She had signed the lease – and she had been promised an electric cooker.

It was a huge task. But Daphne, determined to move in by Christmas, was on home ground: after her earlier residence at Ferryside she knew many of the people who worked in Fowey. She surrounded herself with experts – including her lawyer who, as ever, provided the cold water of reason, and pessimism, which she countered constantly: 'And my answer always "Please, please, see if it can be done".'

Daphne's own description of those months captures the feverish activity: 'The creeper cut from the windows. The windows mended. The men upon the roof mortaring the slates. The carpenter in the house, setting up the doors. The plumber in the well, measuring the water. The electrician on the ladder, wiring the walls.' Doors

and windows were flung open to admit the sunlight that the rooms had been deprived of for so long. 'The sun warming the cold dusty rooms. Fires of brushwood in the grates. And then the scrubbing of the floors that had felt neither brush nor mop for many years. Relays of charwomen, with buckets and swabs. The house alive with women and women. Where did they come from? How did it happen? The whole thing was an impossibility in wartime. Yet it did happen.'

By September the most important work was done. Daphne excitedly told Tod: 'Masons have done the roof (over the bit we shall be in) and the plumbers have got the water pipes in order. The house already looks quite perky and cheerful and I am getting wildly impatient to see it all finished. It's great fun going there and poking round and telling the workmen what to do.'

By the end of the year, remarkably, Menabilly was ready for habitation. Her dream of Christmas at Menabilly would be a

LEFT The dining room at Menabilly. The table, now at Ferryside, first belonged to George du Maurier and was where he drew his cartoons for *Punch*.
ABOVE Frederic Whiting's portrait of Daphne, Jeanne and Angela is now hanging, on loan, in the Lord Speaker's apartment in the House of Lords.

reality. For a second important time, her life was following her fiction. Just as her wedding in 1932 had followed the example of Janet Coombe in *The Loving Spirit*, now, just as the second Mrs de Winter of *Rebecca* had done, she was coming to her Manderley.

Daphne contacted the depositories where she had stored her furniture at the start of the war, rang up removal companies, and arranged dates for delivery. A bout of flu that laid the family low did not thwart her. Chivvied by her, they rose from their sick beds at Readymoney and moved into Menabilly.

A wonderful transformation had been wrought, according to Flavia. Daphne took the children into the room they had seen 'months before with its rotten floor and fallen ceiling. Walls were restored and covered in pretty flowered paper which matched the sofa and chairs. A warm carpet covered the floor and a rocking horse stood prancing, his flared nostrils reflecting the red glare from the fire banked up in the grate. We jumped with joy at the sight of our new nursery.'

One wing had been abandoned, though it provided useful storage space for the rest of the furniture from Cannon Hall; with its empty echoing passages filled with rubble and crumbling plaster where bats roosted, it was strictly out of bounds – and therefore endlessly fascinating to the children. But other rooms had been made habitable and comfortable: the Long Room, as it became known, became a favourite place with its deep chairs and sofas.

The renovation was a triumph. Tommy, who managed to get a week off at Christmas, was astonished to find a house with electric light in all the rooms, telephone installed, fires in all the living rooms, furniture in the places he would have chosen himself and a hot bath waiting. Everything was ready for the festive season, sprays of holly tucked behind the pictures. Daphne's mother and sisters came over for Christmas Day: 'everyone most complimentary', Daphne was pleased to report, though in a letter to Tod sent on New Year's Eve, she admitted to being 'pretty well worn out'; there was much always to do. 'I don't know when we're ever going to get time to sit down as by the time the beds are done and fires lit, it's time for a meal and when that is washed up, it's time for the next.'

The logistics of restoring and keeping such a large house in order were daunting, even with the help of the two young sisters Daphne had employed as well as Margaret, who was in charge of the children and, to begin with, the cooking, but Daphne usefully had priorities: 'Personally the only things that I like bone clean are the bath and the lav pan! It's my theory that endless brushing and dusting is unnecessary, and I'd clean a room once a fortnight!' However, she did get quite exasperated with the untidiness of the children.

She ended her letter with a glimpse into the hectic nature of life: 'I must now rush and cut some wood – bring in some coal

– lay my lunch table – re-light any fires that have gone out – and get Kits out of his leggings, and ready for a meal. What a life. But thank heaven for this lovely old house and mellow peaceful surroundings.'

Improvements continued. Though, characteristically, in her own bedroom Daphne decided to retain the original faded wallpaper of white roses, which made her feel more in touch with the past, the walls by the splendid staircase were painted cream, and on one was hung Frederic Whiting's portrait of the three du Maurier sisters (now on loan to the Government Art Collection, and hanging in the Lord Speaker's apartment in the House of Lords). 'Such an improvement. But I haven't started on the drawing room yet. Tommy's departure rather damped me.'

Window panes were replaced (A.L. Rowse later claimed 'a little credit for encouraging her to get rid of the plate-glass from the front and restore the proper small panes'). Guest rooms were gradually added – Blue Lady (so called because a lady in a blue gown was supposed to have been seen looking out of the window), now graced with electric light, and Little Arthur (named after a Rashleigh). Daphne continued to unpack and install the precious items of her past – the *Punch* drawings and caricatures by her grandfather, the walking sticks from Cannon Hall, and most especially the full-length portrait of her father, the photographs and his bust in bronze. The headed notepaper was ordered, and by Easter the words 'Menabilly, Par, Cornwall' were embossed in scarlet on her favoured cream notepaper.

She could even think of writing again – to begin with short stories, which, despite her happiness in her new home, had morbid or disturbing themes. She quickly established her routine. She would, as usual, have breakfast in bed and by ten o'clock she would be seated at her typewriter at the desk in the alcove of her bedroom, which overlooked the wide lawn. Only Kits was allowed in there while she wrote. Later, a wooden hut was placed at the end of the lawn close by the rhododendrons and overlooking

ABOVE Daphne ordered headed notepaper, with insignia taken from the Browning coat of arms, as soon as she moved into Menabilly. RIGHT Daphne's writing hut, where she kept strict working hours, was at the end of the long lawn and overlooking the sea.

the sea, and she would adjourn there each morning, even in bad weather, wearing jerkin and wellington boots as protection from the elements, until the lunch gong at one o'clock. In the afternoon she would walk, sometimes taking the children. In the evening, she would change for supper – into velvet trousers with a satin blouse or a long embroidered housecoat – which she would take alone and then read the papers by the library fire, or play the

piano. Even in the rather anarchic surroundings of Menabilly, she adhered to the practice of children eating separately, a tradition she maintained from her childhood. She revelled in her solitude.

Despite the isolated location there were occasional interruptions – from Americans, for example, who had arrived en masse in Fowey in preparation for D-Day. Daphne was asked to give a secret party for American war correspondents, so secret that her own staff had to be sent away for the evening, and Muriel and Angela drafted in to act as co-hostesses. Other visits were unscheduled: 'The peace of my garden is rather spoilt at weekends by curious Yanks, in groups of a dozen at a time, coming right up to the house and saying "Say, does the author of *Rebecca* live here?" . . . Notices of Private on the gate have no effect.' Tessa, in a talk she gave to the Daphne du Maurier Festival in 2008, recounted how they would

turn up in their jeeps, asking for autographs, and how she – aged eleven – would be sent out to deal with them, while Daphne disappeared on to the roof, from which she could observe without being seen. Tessa quite enjoyed her task: 'I would explain that my mother had gone out to lunch and would not be back for a long time. When they started coming into the house and wandering round, I was not sure what to do! Eventually, I decided the best approach was to tell them that my mother had just telephoned to say she would not be back unatil after dinner!'

Daphne rarely left Menabilly at this time, though there were occasional excursions, such as birthday outings to the Red Lion in Truro, or to the Troy Cinema in Fowey to see the film of *Frenchman's Creek* after it was released in 1944, when there was a gala night (a treat, but small consolation for the annoying fact

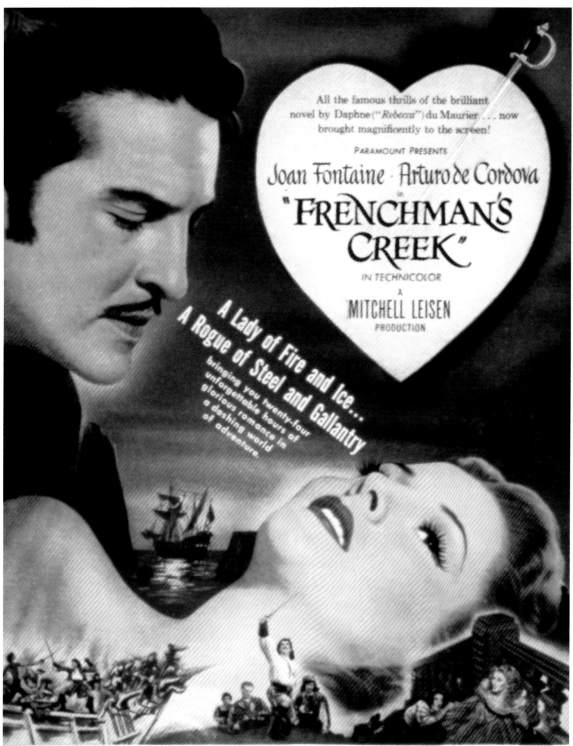

LEFT The 1944 film *Frenchman's Creek* relocated Daphne's story from Cornwall to California, which annoyed her, but enabled her to refurbish Menabilly. OPPOSITE Kits with his boat at the rock pool named Dr Rashleigh's Bath on the beach at Polridmouth.

that the film had been made in California rather than on the Helford River). And she appreciated one visit to London when Tommy was on leave, when they stayed in Claridge's ('ye gods, the bill!) and experienced the comforts of life away from Menabilly: 'It was joy to ring a bell and have it answered, and to eat grouse and pêche melba for supper instead of beans on toast. But I was glad to get back to my own fireside. I do dislike London.'

Daphne relished being in charge of her own life, and some of the ambivalence she had about the return of Tommy after the war, mixed with experience from her own recent life, was aired in a play she wrote: *The Years Between*. All the action takes place in the library of a manor house, perhaps not unlike that at Menabilly, with long windows leading on to a garden. After Colonel Wentworth, a Conservative Member of Parliament, is lost at sea his wife is elected to his seat and then falls in love with an old friend – whereupon Captain Wentworth, who had been secretly and heroically organizing resistance in Europe, reappears. The play was produced at the Opera House, Manchester, on 20 November 1944, and transferred to her father's old theatre, Wyndham's, for a long run, though the reviews were modest.

Meanwhile, there was the difficulty of running Menabilly – a continually haphazard affair. Living in Cornwall with a family, inevitably, did not allow quite the same free and easy lifestyle as before. There was the education of the children to consider. There was no school nearby, and Daphne did not drive, although she could: she had learned on her mother's car when she was twenty. It was as though she revelled in the isolation that this ensured; or perhaps she did not want her routine disrupted by the need to drive the children about. A teacher was found who was prepared to come to Menabilly, but no one was very sorry when she had to give up because of gallstones. In the end, the ideal solution was found when Tod, dear Tod, was persuaded to come and live at Menabilly. Not only would she teach the children until they went to boarding school, but she could also manage the house.

This would leave Daphne free to work. Everyone would be happy, Daphne thought, as she had convinced herself that the children loved the vast spaces of the house and garden.

Looking back, the children have mixed views. Kits 'loved the grounds. I was not so mad about the house.' The house was frightening: 'Kits and I used to walk hand in hand up the stairs,' said Flavia; they wouldn't go up at all unless all the lights were on. Bats would come in and fly round, and there was often the sound of rats scurrying overhead – though Daphne would tell them stories about the rats, which made them laugh. And it was cold. Always bitterly cold. The stacked-up fires in the living

Daphne du Maurier at Home

rooms, supplemented by paraffin stoves or one-bar electric fires, made little impact in the depths of winter. Complaints from the children were met with 'go and put on another jersey'. At the start of 1947, the coldest winter of the century, the children went to bed in their clothes and with two water bottles apiece.

The grounds were a different matter, and they enjoyed long walks with Daphne through the exotic woods with their ferns, bamboos and cork trees, which had once been the talk of the world. The Cornish naturalist William Borlase noted (in 1727) that 'every thing that belongs to the flower-garden, and grows in any part of England, will thrive and flourish here'. Now it was barely kept under control, though Mr Burt, who came in from the nearest hamlet of Hamelin, did his best. In 1951 Nicholas Pevsner commented that Menabilly's gardens had been 'with its wealth of tropical plants unparalleled in Britain'. Paths led everywhere, and the children gave them names, such as Palm Walk and Creepy

OPPOSITE Though she loved her privacy, Daphne had to endure occasional photo shoots for publicity purposes – in this case for *The Sketch* in 1944. ABOVE Family portrait posed on the side lawn of Menabilly.

Walk (because of the yew trees). Happy Valley, so named in *Rebecca*, really was full of azaleas in the spring, and the woods were full of snowdrops, daffodils, bluebells and wild garlic. 'The whole of Mena stank of wild garlic,' remembers Flavia.

And there were the excursions down to the sea. Daphne swam every day, sometimes twice a day, from May to September. There were picnics on Polridmouth Beach, and playing in the rock pools, including one dubbed Dr Rashleigh's Bath, which was ideal for floating boats on. As Polridmouth Beach was a public beach, the

ABOVE Flavia, Tessa, Daphne and Kits in 1943 at Polridmouth Cove, a favourite spot for picnics and bathing.
OPPOSITE The house on the edge of Polridmouth Cove was the inspiration for the boathouse in *Rebecca*.

family would often opt for the seclusion of Long Chops Corner, their name for a little inlet with a rocky spit, below the path to the Gribbin, to which they could scramble. There was still the carcass of a cargo ship, the wrecking of which in the early 1930s had given Daphne the idea for part of the plot of *Rebecca*.

And here was Rebecca's boathouse. Actually once a mill house, it is now a solid four-bedroom house. For years it was the weekend retreat of a businessman, Ron Diggens, who used to fly down to the cottage in his own plane, which he would land on a field by Coombe Farm just up from the cove. He spent a lot of money on the house, rather as Daphne did on Menabilly, laid crazy paving and terraces, and landscaped the whole area next to the millpond,

on which there seemed always to be a pair of swans – 'there have always been two swans', said Flavia – which provided inspiration for Daphne's short story 'The Old Man'.

Nearby was a grotto, constructed in the eighteenth century by Philip Rashleigh and composed of enormous sea pebbles and shells, with an octagonal table made of thirty-one specimens of Cornish granite and walls covered with 'Cornish minerals, crystals, agates, and shells from all over the world'. There was once a custodian: old guidebooks recount how one could get a key from the nearby cottage, and even perhaps 'a good plain tea'. But the grotto has tumbled down and the minerals are now gone.

There were other residents too: Miss Phillips and Miss Willcox, who rather alarmed the children, lived at Southcott Cottage, in a clearing just off the old drive. Captain Vandeleur, who was the agent for the Rashleighs, lived in a wooden house overlooking the sea and grew camellias. He also used to cut bamboo from the grounds to send to London Zoo for the pandas.

The family did not have the woods to themselves. Captain Vanderleur had given permission for Boy Scouts to use a hut, which was hung with hammocks, and to roam around the woods. David Rowan, now a retired teacher, was one of those boys, and he vividly recollects his times at Menabilly. Once, a group of the boys met a man on the path who invited them up to the house for tea. It was Tommy. Being only seven, what David was interested in was the array of bows and arrows by the door, but he also remembers a woman presiding at the tea table – not Daphne, but Tod.

One other memory stands out: 'There were two boys playing on the lawn, with bikes, I think. And one of our group, older than me, said, "You see him [the one who was not Kits]? He's a viscount!" Whether he was or not, I don't know, but there we were, boys hiding in trees on the edge of the lawn, like a tribe, on the edge of this oasis of grandeur.'

For Daphne, it was not the grandeur that was important but the essence, the spirit of the house, with which she so identified.

When she was commissioned to write the leading article for a book called *Countryside Character*, published in 1946, she described her feelings about the house in 'The House of Secrets':

From the end of the lawn where I first saw her, that May morning, I stand and look upon her face. The ivy is stripped. Smoke curls from the chimney, the windows are flung wide. The doors are open. My children come running from the house on to the lawn. The hydrangeas bloom for me. Clumps of them stand on my piano.

It's wrong, I think, to love a block of stone like this, as one loves a person. It cannot last. It cannot endure. Perhaps it is the very insecurity of the love that makes the passion strong. Because she is not mine by right. The house is still entailed, and one day will belong to another.

I brush the thought aside. For this day, and for this night, she is mine. And at midnight, when the children sleep, and all is hushed and still, I sit down at the piano and look at the panelled walls, and slowly, softly, with no one there to see, the house whispers her secrets, and the secrets turn to stories; in a strange and eerie fashion, we are one, the house and I.

Chapter 6
LIVING AT MENABILLY

The first novel Daphne wrote when she was living at Menabilly was about Menabilly. It was as though the house really had whispered its secrets to her. Whereas in *Rebecca*, Manderley was Menabilly on the outside but Milton on the inside, *The King's General* showed Menabilly inside and out.

Daphne had long been fascinated by the story of a bricked-up room in a buttress wall at Menabilly, discovered in 1824. Inside was, as she explained in the postscript to her novel, the skeleton of a young man, seated on a stool, a trencher at this feet, and the skeleton was dressed in the clothes of a Cavalier, as worn during the Civil War. Menabilly, a stronghold of the Royalist Rashleighs, had been sacked by the Parliamentarians in 1648. Now she was *in situ*, she could set her imagination free. But first she needed a solid background of fact. She wanted her story to be as close to the historical background as possible. And something

Daphne looking up at the buttress where there was a bricked-up room containing a skeleton, found in 1824, which inspired her eighth novel, *The King's General*.

Daphne was good at, and took a pride in, was research.

She contacted the Rashleighs to ask if she could see some of the family papers, and stumbled at the first hurdle. Though Dr Rashleigh sent her a 'fascinating' map of the house as it was in 1740, other papers and manuscripts that she needed to make the story authentic were in the keeping of the heir apparent and he refused to lend them to her. 'I may snooker him and get A.L. Rowse to lend me the copies, which are in the Cornish Institution,' Daphne wrote.

However, her determination won the day, and in her acknowledgments she thanked the Rashleigh family for giving her permission to print 'this blend of fact and fiction'. Members of the Rashleigh family feature as characters, along with other contemporary figures, such as the Grenville family and Lord Robartes of Lanhydrock, the grand estate near Bodmin. (Only the fine gatehouse remains from the seventeenth century: the mansion was rebuilt in Victorian times.) She took the name of Honor Harris, the strong main character and narrator, from a plaque in the church in Tywardreath (which is where Honor's home is when telling this story). Honor's fictional family, the

ABOVE A photograph taken by Tommy of the grounds of Menabilly in the snow, with Gribbin Head in the background.
RIGHT This plaque in Tywardreath Church gave Daphne the name of Honor Harris, the narrator in *The King's General*.

Harrises of Lanrest, is exact in fact: the father was John, her sisters Mary and Cecily (Cecilia in *The King's General*), who married John Pollexfen; her elder brother Christopher (Kit) married Gertrude (Gartred), daughter of Sir Bernard Grenville of Stow. Daphne was thorough in her research.

One even feels, on reading the account of the pillage by the Parliamentary troops, that she must have read *A Historical Survey of the County of Cornwall*, in which the losses, as itemized by Jonathan Rashleigh, were 500 sheep, 100 lambs, 18 draught oxen, 20 milch cows, 30 fatted bullocks, 60 store bullocks, 40 horses and 8 hogs, a whole year's supply of butter, cheese, beer, wine, beef, pork and bacon as well as corn and 'my hay, grasses, gardens, orchards all spoyled'.

More striking even than the book's faith to the historical background is its powerful portrayal of the moors and coast of Cornwall. From its opening words *The King's General* illustrates the sensitivity for the Cornish landscape and the minute observation derived from her long walks that characterize so much of Daphne's fiction:

September, 1653. The last of summer. The first chill winds of autumn. The sun no longer strikes my eastern window

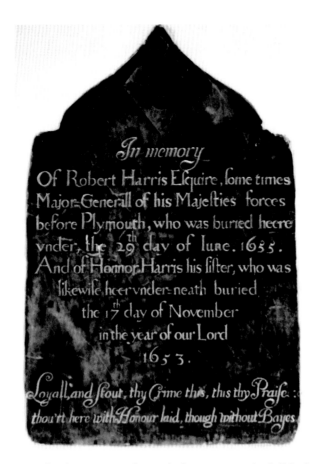

In memory

Of Robert Harris Efquire, fome times
Major Generall of his Majefties forces
before Plymouth, who was buried heere
vnder, the 29th day of Iune. 1655.
And of Honnor Harris his fifter, who was
likewife heer vnder-neath buried
the 17th day of November
in the year of our Lord
1653.

Loyall, and ftout, thy Crime this, this thy Praife. :
thou'rt here with Honour laid, though without Bayes.

The action of the book ranges across Cornwall from Launceston Castle and Lanhydrock to Lanrest, Honor's childhood home above the East Looe River, which Daphne renders evocatively: 'Even now, thirty years after, I have only to close my eyes and think of home, and there comes to my nostrils the well-remembered scent of hay, hot with the sun, blown by a lazy wind; and I see the great wheel thrashing the water down at the mills at Lemetton, and I smell the fusty, dusty golden grain. The sky was always white with pigeons . . .'

But at the heart of the novel is Menabilly, from its 'long gallery, a great dark panelled chamber with windows looking out on to the court and eastward to the gardens' to Gribbin hill, which watches 'in every mood from winter to midsummer'. The extensive description of Gribbin Head (quoted in an essay by Sheila Hodges, Daphne's editor, who felt that she was not given enough credit for her descriptions of nature) demonstrates well Daphne's skill in turning real-life experience into fiction.

as I wake, but, turning laggard, does not top the hill before eight o'clock. A white mist hides the bay sometimes until noon, and hangs about the marshes too, leaving, when it lifts, a breath of cold air behind it. Because of this, the tall grass in the meadow never dries, but long past midday shimmers and glistens in the sun, the great drops of moisture hanging motionless upon the stems. I notice the tides more than I did once. They seem to make a pattern to the day. When the water drains from the marshes, and little by little the yellow sands appear, rippling and hard and firm, it seems to my foolish fancy, as I lie here, that I too go seaward with the tide, and all my own hidden dreams that I thought buried for all time are bare and naked to the day, just as the shells and the stones are on the sands.

The sea is very white and still, without a breath upon it, and only a single thread of wash upon the covered Cannis rock. The jackdaws fly homewards to their nests in the warren. The sheep crop the short turf, before they too rub together beneath the stone wall by the winnowing place. Dusk comes slowly to the Gribbin hill, the woods turn black, and suddenly, with stealthy pad, a fox creeps from the trees in the thistle park, and stands watching me, his ears pricked . . . Then his brush twitches and he is gone.

At the beginning of this passage is a heartfelt invocation from Honor: 'God bless the Rashleighs, who permitted me those months at Menabilly. The house was bare and shorn of its former glory . . .' That could be Daphne speaking as herself. It must have been exhilarating for her to write *The King's General* about the Rashleighs when she was so connected to them, about the effects

Tommy, whose job as Treasurer to Prince Philip kept him in London, spent his weekends in Cornwall in the open air, sailing and walking.

the end of 1944 he had been despatched to the Far East as Chief of Staff to Lord Mountbatten. In her letters to Tod, Daphne had been anxious about where he might be posted after his return, and whether she might be expected to follow the role of military wife again. 'I wish I didn't feel so much on the edge of a precipice living here. It would really break my heart to go.' But his new post was in London as Military Secretary to the Secretary of State for War and she was safe in her resolution to remain in Menabilly – and to retain control of her own life. One indication of that was that Tommy now had a separate bedroom.

Tommy, who was knighted in 1946 (Daphne ordered correspondence cards inscribed 'Lady Browning'), would work in London during the week, staying in the flat in Whitelands House close to Sloane Square, which he had taken over from his sister Grace. It was a rather comfortless two-bedroom flat, occasionally also used by Daphne, though she disliked it intensely (when she had to stay there for an extended period later, she called it 'the Rat Trap'). In 1948 Tommy resigned from the army and became Comptroller General to the Household of Princess Elizabeth and the Duke of Edinburgh. He was well known to Princess Elizabeth: her first official military title was as Colonel of the Grenadier Guards, when she was appointed by her father in 1942 on her sixteenth birthday, and Tommy had attended her first inspection of the troops at Windsor Castle. After she became Queen, Tommy became Treasurer to Prince Philip, a prestigious position though not a lucrative one.

Tommy would come down to Cornwall on the sleeper train on Friday night, reversing the journey on the Sunday night. His weekends were packed with activities with and without the family: archery, sailing on *Fanny Rosa*, the boat he had brought back from Singapore, and drawing up plans for new boats. He and Tessa might sail their Troy, *Shimmer*. When Hunkin's boatyard came up for sale, Daphne bought it for Tommy. She could afford to: *The King's General* had sold over a million copies in three weeks, and

of Civil War on a place where there was still tangible evidence of it, and about Menabilly while she was living there.

The King's General, with its ambiguous dedication 'To My Husband, also a general, but, I trust, a more discreet one', was published in 1946, the year Tommy came back to England: at

the film rights (though the film was never made) were sold for £65,000, imbuing her with a sure sense of financial security.

But she could not have the one thing she wanted more than anything. If only she could buy Menabilly. Echoing the words she had once written in her diary about Fowey ('It's much more than love for a person'), she wrote to a friend, 'I do believe I love Mena more than people.' But the estate was entailed, and so could not be sold and, by law, must pass to a member of the family. Constant anxiety about her tenancy was a continuing theme in her correspondence, and she kept up the pressure on her landlord. Only months after she had moved she was fretting: 'No hint of old man Rashleigh giving me an extended lease. I've just got to pray he lives for ever.' It was a plea she was to reiterate when she started worrying not about Dr Rashleigh but about his heir: 'I keep hearing in roundabout ways that he can hardly wait to step in. My only hope is for the old doctor to live for ever. I trembled for him in this cold spell!'

Daphne had hoped to charm 'the Heir', but he sounded 'even more tricky than the old doctor. And for two pins would step in now, I believe, if he could, (me having made the improvements).' Later, she told Tod of the personal tragedy that had afflicted him: his son, a soldier in the Coldstream Guards, had been shot and was seriously ill, and his parents were at his bedside. Though Daphne had sympathy for them, she was also anxious about the possible consequence for her life at Menabilly: 'What happens if the poor lad dies? I'm wondering what effect it will have . . . it might make the heir lose interest, or make him feel Menabilly was the only thing left now in the world. I feel on tenterhooks.'

But in 1947 she had another concern: life at Menabilly was disrupted when a lawsuit was brought against her in New York for plagiarism in *Rebecca*. She had to go to America, where she stayed for three months. Tessa was now at boarding school, and she took Kits and Flavia with her, along with Tod. They stayed with her American publisher, Nelson Doubleday, and his wife,

Ellen, whose glamour and kindness immediately endeared her to Daphne. She depended on Ellen utterly in the ordeal of the trial, which dragged on for weeks, though ended in her exoneration. They arrived back home just before Christmas, when Daphne took to her bed, wrung out with nervous exhaustion.

Perhaps Daphne had hoped for more from Ellen – Tessa felt that her mother became 'besotted' with her – but they remained good friends. And, as was so often the case, the friendship provided inspiration for a play, *September Tide,* which tells the story of a middle-aged woman whose artist son-in-law falls in love with her. It was set, recognizably, at Ferryside, which in the play became 'Stella Martyn's house on a Cornish estuary'. The actress chosen for the part of Stella was one already known to Daphne: Gertrude Lawrence, just nine years older than Daphne, had been Gerald's last leading lady, in *Behold, We Live* by John Van Druten in 1932. For Daphne, who knew well of her father's dalliances, and whose feelings about her father were complex and suppressed, this must have been a peculiar turn of events; that unique connection would have ensured that she felt a particular bond with Gertrude. Daphne told Sheridan Morley, when he was researching his biography of Gertrude, 'I remembered that Gerald, my father, always gave his leading ladies presents and took them to lunch at the Savoy. I must do the same . . . I do recollect presents of champagne, a fur rug . . . so to some extent I was doing a Gerald.' Their shared sense of humour and fun cemented the friendship for Daphne, who spent time in loathed London to be with her – and even flew across the Atlantic (something she loathed nearly as much) to see her and to discuss the play she was planning to write for her. Gertrude's sudden death from cancer in 1952 shocked Daphne greatly. She wrote later to Oriel Malet, a young writer she met at about the same time at a publishing party, that it took her about four years to 'get over that thing of Gertrude dying, and she was *not* a person who filled my whole life . . . but a lovely illusion'.

That play was to have been about another of Daphne's

noteworthy ancestors, Mary Anne, her great-great-grandmother and mistress of the Duke of York. Instead, Daphne used the material later for a novel published in 1954, *Mary Anne*, though she found it hard work and did not enjoy the result. As her editor Sheila Hodges later pointed out, it contained what might well be a *cri de coeur*: 'My God, a woman can be lonely when she's the one to earn the daily bread.'

Much-needed diversion was provided by a trip to Greece, and to consult the Delphic oracle, with Clara Vyvyan, despite the reservations Daphne had expressed about travel with Clara: 'She is prepared to sleep in a haystack but I don't think I am.' The difficulty was 'my awful ritual of creaming my face, and my hair in pins, and breakfast in bed! Obviously I must rid myself of these foibles. How ease of life does creep into one's bones.' But she had, a couple of years earlier, walked part of the way with Clara on her expedition along the length of the Rhône. She was, wrote Clara in her memoir, the best of companions:

> sometimes content with hours of silence, and then suddenly pouring out the overflow of a rich mind. She could dramatize a stone, invest the Gregorian chanting of a priest with pagan significance, and read a whole history in the wrinkles of some old crone. I can see her now, perched on a mid-stream boulder that divided the current of a high-Alpine river, listening quietly for hours to the torrent, as she rode her own private Pegasus through her own self-created purgatory or heaven or hell . . . She had a puckish sense of humour. Often round a simple jest, heard or uttered, she will accumulate, as it were, a rolling snowball, more and more material, until she has produced a wild extravaganza.

The trip to Greece was entertaining, but it did not lead to any new thoughts for a book, which was frustrating. *Mary Anne*,

disappointing as it was, had marked the end of a particularly productive period. Between 1949 and 1951, Daphne had written three books: *The Parasites*, about a richly gifted and bohemian family, with echoes of her own family and regarded as one of her funniest books; a book of letters and sketches on her grandfather, *The Young George du Maurier*; and *My Cousin Rachel*, partly prompted by seeing a picture at Antony House in Cornwall of Rachel Carew, who married Ambrose Manaton, just as Rachel married Ambrose in *My Cousin Rachel*. This novel too was set on her doorstep, with one of her typically dramatic openings: 'They used to hang men at Four Turnings in the old days.'

Here, in *My Cousin Rachel*, are the rhododendrons, the camellia plantation, the mill cottage on the beach, the pony's paddock by the lawn, the favoured spots for swimming – all known to Daphne so well in her daily life. The Rashleigh monument that Daphne and Flavia had discovered together, with its coat of arms and inscriptions, plays a part. And so, though unnamed, does Menabilly, encircled by trees – surely the mansion which Philip Ashley (not such a distant name from Rashleigh) cherished: it 'lay in a sort of saucer, but already the trees planted . . . grew thick and fast to give the house more shelter, and to the north the new avenue wound though the woods and up the rise to where the four roads met.' And there are the views and sounds that Daphne must have heard at her home:

> The long lawns dipped to the meadows and the meadows to the sea . . . The trees that fringed the lawns were black and still. Rabbits came out and pricked about the grass, then scattered to their burrows; and the bark of a vixen, with the little sob that follows it, eerie and unmistakable, unlike any other call that comes by night, and out of the woods, I saw the lean low body creep and run out upon the lawn, and hide again where the trees would cover it.

Gertrude Lawrence, Gerald du Maurier's last leading lady in 1932, was the star in Daphne's 1949 play *September Tide*, which was set in Ferryside.

DAPHNE DU MAURIER AT HOME

The narrator of *My Cousin Rachel* is as passionate about his domain as Daphne was about hers – even though it was not actually hers. She wrote in the first person, as she often did, which gave her the chance to weave a story as well as express her own feelings. The boundaries between the two were often hard to define. 'When one is writing a novel in the first person, one must be that person,' she said more than once. 'I can think much better as an "I".' There is a sense in which the fantasy was often more real to her than daily life. Flavia recounted how at mealtimes Daphne,

> if she were brewing on a story, would sit at her end of the table, picking at her food and staring into space, a vacant look on her face. My father would suddenly pounce and ask her a question: 'Well, what do you think, Duck?' (They called each other Duck.) She would drag herself back to the present: 'Well, I can hardly say, Duck,' she would reply, a faint smile on her face. My father would look down the table at her and thunder, 'Woman, you live in a dream!' which indeed she did when working hard on some novel or other.

Her 'routes' were devised wholly to allow the muse the freedom to work. Her discipline in writing at set times every day was as much an indulgence in the imaginary world she was inhabiting. The long walks were an opportunity to continue in that world.

There were, inevitably, interruptions. There were occasional official engagements that she had to fulfil with Tommy because of his role in the Royal Household, including the ordeal, for Daphne, of a visit to Balmoral (though she admitted to finding the company of the Queen Mother very relaxing). She was always

Photograph of Daphne taken soon after she moved to Menabilly by Dorothy Wilding, later famous for her portraits of the Queen, which were used on postage stamps.

anxious about her clothes for such engagements, though in fact, according to Flavia, she had some beautiful dresses in the London flat. 'She could look gorgeous. She had a smart hairdresser, and a beautician would visit to give her a facial and to do her make up.' Even when wearing trousers, back in Cornwall, she could be quite particular: 'She loved belts. Perhaps it was part of being boyish.'

There was no entertaining at home, unlike the Sunday lunch parties given by her parents. When Ellen Doubleday announced her intention of visiting, Daphne was thrown into a panic, remembering the luxury of Barberrys, Ellen's home on Long Island, and feeling the Blue Lady guest room would be inadequate. But Tod rose to the occasion, organizing its refurbishment, even to the extent of adding a bathroom. Oriel Malet, who stayed in Blue Lady, described it (perhaps after its facelift) as 'a cheerful and welcoming room', its white-painted walls hung with *Punch* sketches by George du Maurier, offset by a deep crimson carpet and chintz curtains patterned with famous ships framed by garlands of oak leaves.

There was more stress when Prince Philip came to stay one night in 1950, an event that thoroughly alarmed everyone. Daphne wrote that 'Tommy is getting Prince Philip panic and polishing things, and decanting port,' adding 'we've only got four knives that aren't bust, and one silver candlestick must be glued!' Flavia remembers the difficulty of curtseying to Prince Philip in corduroy trousers, and later glimpsing him in the Long Room. 'He kept picking up magazines, flipping them open and putting them down. He was rather restless.' There was even more of a kerfuffle when the Queen visited in July 1962. Luckily it was after Daphne had finished writing her latest book, *The Glass-Blowers*, inspired by her glass-making forebears, but she was distraught: 'It is the Doom of all time . . . It means a commotion, and all her entourage, and policemen and chauffeurs – how *shall* we manage it? It has ruined my summer!'

Daphne's main contribution to this domestic upheaval was

ABOVE The Queen and Prince Philip on board Tommy's boat, *Fanny Rosa*. (Tommy has his back to the camera).
RIGHT Tommy and Daphne walking down the long lawn away from Menabilly.

filling the flower vases. It was the only housework that she ever enjoyed: she always kept the vases filled – all twenty-six of them. She would scour the grounds for blooms and branches, even to the extent of raiding Captain Vandeleur's camellia plantation. At Christmas, she would twine ivy and holly through the balusters of the staircase and tuck sprays behind the pictures. She had no interest in gardening herself, but was glad that Tod did. One letter to Tod when she was away from Menabilly gives an indication of her preferences for cut flowers, as she reported on Tod's garden: 'Your cos lettuce is coming on well now we have had some rain', but then went on to the more interesting topic of rating the flowers: the gladioli were 'looking fine and are coming in well

for the tall glass by my chair in the Long Room'. Marigolds and daisies were also good for the Long Room, as were lupins and sweet peas. Sweet peas were 'a lifesaver for the bedrooms'. Nasturtiums 'though a heavenly colour, don't last long in this stuffy weather for the centre vase'. And dahlias, 'though glorious in bloom unpicked, droop when brought to the house'.

LIVING AT MENABILLY

Daphne was never wholly content unless she had a story brewing, another world to enter into. But though that element of play-acting was so crucial, the actual composition was all important too. Sheila Hodges said Daphne was 'a very careful craftsman', and described how she took great care over the endings of chapters. She wrote to Victor Gollancz once in some frustration, telling him that she had taken two mornings over the last line of *Mary Anne* (which ended '. . . and watching a million starlings span the sky'), yet 'people think I "dash off" my novels'.

She would have liked more recognition for her talents, and admitted to minding about bad or lukewarm reviews: 'The fact that I sold well in the past, never really made up for them. Of course making money has been very useful, because of being able to afford Mena, and bring up the children, but I somehow don't connect money-making with the writing, not in my mind.' She kept an eye on the success of established writers, such as Agatha Christie, whom she knew slightly, and whose paperbacks, she noted on a trip to France, sold well in translation, and newcomers: 'There is a new person who has taken over from me called Mary Stewart, who sells a lot. I don't now.' Income and reputation were things which she remained conscious of, and sometimes anxious about, for the rest of her life.

But, high sales or not, good or bad reviews, Daphne needed to write. She was always alert for an idea, which might come from anywhere.

famous when Hitchcock based his 1963 film *The Birds* on it.

An encounter on a trip to France with her younger sister, Jeanne, and Jeanne's friend Noel Welch gave her the idea for *The Scapegoat,* which meshed with her growing interest in psychology and the question of identity: Flavia relates the conversations that they would have about Jung and Adler on long walks. After the novel was published in 1957, there was talk of a film, which led to a friendship with Sir Alec Guinness and a visit to his house in Petersfield in Hampshire, which, Daphne noted, was very new, 'like in adverts of *Ladies' Home Journal,* very American and labour-saving. I am sure they adore it, and it was very nice, but it made me long for shabby old Mena.'

For a while in 1957 Daphne tried to live in London, after a crisis when Tommy had a breakdown. She wanted to look after him and to keep him company, but she found it impossible to work at the flat, and claustrophobic – this was when she dubbed it the Rat Trap. At one point in early 1958, she thought of renting another house, next to an archery ground – which sounded very suitable for Tommy – but her enthusiasm died when she realized that nowhere would be a substitute for Menabilly. And Tommy was unwilling to pay for it. He 'did not want to fork out from his Trust to pay. That's the awful bitter thing. I have provided for *all* of them, and have no capital myself.'

While in London she had one, slightly sour, pleasure: that of painting the view from the bedroom. 'I made it all strident and screaming, because of my hate, with glaring chimneypots, and those awful Power Station Battersea things, belching evil smoke.' At that difficult time, her writing hut at Menabilly became, for a brief spell, an artist's studio, when she turned to oil painting as a release from her worries.

Tommy retired in 1959 to live at Menabilly all the time, and they recovered their old camaraderie, enjoying television together (they watched *Coronation Street* from the first episodes, and Tommy loved *Grandstand*), and listening to records of

LEFT 'The Birds' was published in the 1952 short-story collection *The Apple Tree*, but became more famous after Hitchcock based his 1963 film *The Birds* on it.
ABOVE Daphne used this group photograph of Kits, Tessa and Flavia to illustrate her Christmas card of 1949.

A walk across a stubble field at nearby Menabilly Barton with Oriel, 'while a crowd of seagulls wheeled and cried above us', led Daphne to say suddenly: 'I've often thought how nanny [frightening] it would be if all the birds in the world were to gang up together and attack us. They could, you know.' 'The Birds' was published in the short-story collection *The Apple Tree* in 1952, but became more

Daphne outside her writing hut with Flavia and grandchildren Paul, Rupert and Marie-Thérèse. (Rupert is Flavia's son, and Paul and Marie-Thérèse are Tessa's children.)

American musicals, which they both loved. There were occasional expeditions – including a happy trip to Ireland for the wedding of Kits and Olive in 1962 – and frequent long walks. When Foy Quiller-Couch asked Daphne if she would complete her father's half-written novel *Castle Dor* – based on the Tristan and Iseult legend – she and Tommy together retraced the footsteps of Tristan, Iseult and King Mark in the local Cornish landscape, including the Iron Age hill fort of Castle Dore.

This commission was an unusual challenge for Daphne. Q had planned the novel in 1925 when he came across proof that he was right in his estimation of where King Mark's Castle stood: he refashioned the Tristan and Iseult legend as a romance between the wife of an innkeeper and a Breton onion-seller and set it in his own beloved Troytown. As Rowse said in his memoir of Sir Arthur Quiller-Couch, 'it begins beautifully with its evocation of this lovely countryside, parish of St Sampson of Golant', and Daphne believed the story was worth preserving 'for his description of Fowey countryside alone'. As usual, she applied herself to research, reading widely all the Tristan and Iseult legends, and resolving inconsistencies to satisfy her sense of order. But she was,

DAPHNE DU MAURIER AT HOME

naturally, apprehensive about taking on Q's mantle: as she said in an article for *The Sunday Telegraph*, reproduced as a preface to the 1979 Pan paperback edition of the book, it seemed presumptuous 'and a bare-faced intrusion upon the silence of the grave'. But she had agreed, as she wanted to please Foy and to 'relive, in memory, happy evenings long ago when "Q" was host at Sunday suppers'. By dint of this, and by reading it again and again, she felt she did find his mood and tone, and that 'by thinking back to conversations long forgotten' she could recapture something of the man – 'rambling, whimsical, suddenly intuitive or alternately obstinate, warmly hospitable, shy for no reason'. Her efforts were a tribute to his support long ago.

Foy sent Rowse a copy with a diffident note, saying 'I fear your censure over this', but Rowse magnanimously withheld that, saying merely that, after all, Q had finished *St Ives*, a book left by his literary hero Robert Louis Stevenson. In fact, the result was a seamless collaboration. It was published by J.M. Dent, rather than Victor Gollancz, and when Daphne sent a copy to Sheila Hodges, she asked if Sheila could spot the join, which was 'at the end of a chapter – but which chapter?' Sheila guessed wrongly, and received a postcard saying 'Hurrah!'

As time went on, Daphne made more trips away, some for holidays, some for reconnaissance. A visit to Haworth, for example, led eventually to *The Infernal World of Branwell Brontë* (she had been long been intrigued that the mother of the Brontës came from Penzance). One trip to Italy with Tessa gave her an idea for *The Flight of the Falcon*. But the creative juices were not quite as much on tap as before. She had difficulty getting 'the feel' of the novel. The ability to call down the atmosphere had receded; in the old days she could shut herself off from everyday inconvenient reality, but that was not always so easy now.

And there were difficult times. The anxiety over Menabilly had resurfaced. In 1948 there had been a plan to buy Ethy House in nearby Lerryn, perhaps instigated by Tommy as it was a favourite spot of his, as a fall-back – 'an alternative weapon', Daphne called it. But when she was told that Cornwall County Council was determined to get it for its agricultural land, she was relieved, as she thought it would have cost too much. And, anyway, what she wanted was to live out her days in Menabilly.

Ten years later, she returned to the fray over the lease of Menabilly, pressing Dr Rashleigh to extend it. To her joy she was successful, but in 1960, before the lease could be signed, Dr Rashleigh died. The new owner was Philip Rashleigh (the young soldier son of 'the Heir', whose life-threatening injuries at the end of the war had caused Daphne such concern; 'the Heir' himself had died suddenly in 1957), who refused to sign it. Desperate for the house she loved, she consulted lawyers and exploited public opinion. Eventually in 1961 Philip capitulated, to the extent of allowing her to stay another seven years. But she was living on borrowed time. It was clear that he definitely intended to move to Cornwall, and she reluctantly agreed to consider the alternative of Kilmarth, the dower house of the Menabilly estate. She went with Tommy to look around it and they were encouraged. Tommy, in particular, felt very positive about Kilmarth, and in 1964 signed the lease.

In the early part of the following year, illness was afflicting them both. Tommy's left leg had been causing him huge pain, and at the start of 1965 his left foot was amputated. Daphne got jaundice and had barely recovered when on 14 March Tommy died. His ashes were scattered at the end of the garden where he and Daphne walked together. Perhaps it was even the spot that she had – years before – selected for her own grave. Her move to Kilmarth would be alone.

CHAPTER 7
FROM SERVANTS TO STAFF

Daphne's earliest memories, as she recounted in the opening words of *Growing Pains*, were of the details of the clothes of the servants of a well-to-do home: Nurse Rush dressed in grey with a black bonnet with a veil; Ellison, the parlourmaid, wearing a cream-coloured uniform, with a frilly cap and apron.

The contrast between those recollections and the night in 1969 when Daphne lent her housekeeper, Esther, her 'best fur coat' to go to a dance encapsulates the change in her households, and mirrors the huge shift that took place during the twentieth century. In her foreword to *Letters from a Cornish Garden* by her friend Clara Vyvyan, when she describes her first visit to Clara's home, Trelowarren, in the late 1920s, she seemed even then to be conscious of the growing anachronism of 'a housemaid, wearing a cap with streamers, who brought hot water in a copper can to my bedroom'. By the time she was living at Menabilly and Kilmarth, there were no housemaids as such; there was always someone to cook – Daphne just didn't, ever. There was a nanny, who left soon after the move to Menabilly; there was eventually a housekeeper. There were cleaners, and, much later, companions and nurses. But there were no servants.

From her youngest days, Daphne was used to a substantial household, and to being waited on. Then, a life separate from parents was the norm in middle-class families: at Cumberland Terrace, the children lived and ate in the nursery in the charge of Nanny, who left soon after Jeanne was born, and a nursemaid, and then Norland nurses, who took her and her sisters for walks in Regent's Park. They had a governess, Miss Torrance. There were two housemaids, and there was a cook, Alice. When they moved to Cannon Hall, the staff was even bigger.

Angela, in her memoir *Old Maids Remember*, recalls vividly the extent of how even the children were ministered to: 'I used to toss off my silk stockings to be darned, and gloves to be washed to a housemaid. Even one's clothes were put away for one.' Daphne, typically, was more concerned with the freedom of the different arrangements at Cannon Hall, when there was 'no longer a nurse to supervise but a children's maid, whose orders we could disregard'.

This picture of a corner of the library at Menabilly, with its glimpse of the nursery, was painted by Tod, Daphne's governess, who came to live at Menabilly in 1944.

When the family went to Mullion Cove – the holiday that was interrupted by Gerald's disaffection with the weather – the children had been left with a full complement of nurse, nanny and governess to take care of them. Had they not been, Daphne would have been deprived of the thrill of the pilchard shoal arriving, the cries of the 'huer' (as the lookout was called), the sight of the boats launching to capture the seething mass of fish: such a night-time expedition would never have been allowed if the parents had been there. Another window into another world

was opened by Dorothy Sheppard, the children's maid at Cannon Hall, who was just six years older than Daphne. She slept in the night nursery with the two younger girls, who cross-examined her on a daily basis about her life and the world outside; Daphne treated her as a friend (and they stayed in touch with each other into old age). But Daphne's life generally at that time was surrounded, constrained and observed by servants.

So for Daphne to look after herself at Ferryside was a real and enjoyable novelty, which enhanced her sense of freedom. And she

GROWING PAINS
— THE SHAPING OF A WRITER —

DAPHNE DU MAURIER

LEFT Tod's painting of the Long Room at Menabilly, with the chair James Barrie used when visiting the du Mauriers, was used for a Christmas card.
ABOVE Daphne's memoir *Growing Pains* recounts the importance of the servants in her childhood.

was prepared to put up with some discomfort: she was always, as she put it when she moved to Readymoney Cove, prepared to 'pig' it. Her increased independence, however, did not, even then, give her a taste for catering for herself, even if, on occasion, she might have done the shopping. Daphne never exhibited any interest in the creative aspects of the culinary arts, and anyway preferred straightforward food – 'Lamb cutlets, grilled sole, for example,' said Flavia. 'And she'd much prefer peaches out of a tin as opposed to some elaborate pudding – though she was very keen on Cornish cream.' Tessa recounted Daphne's wry comment: 'The trouble with cooking is I find it so difficult to open the tins.' She did, however, take great pleasure in her daughter's achievements in that area. 'She was thrilled: she would tell friends "Tessa can make an omelette!"'

And the priority for Daphne was always her inner world. Occasionally, she would regretfully acknowledge her 'inadequacy in domestic life', and she thought Tessa and Flavia might do much better 'because of their more natural feeling, but it *does* take time to think about it, and at the moment I'm in the vault of a bank in La Ferté Bernard, looking for a Marriage Settlement, and I really can't attend to anything else!'

Altogether running the household was always something of an *ad hoc* arrangement. Tommy could never quite understand why Daphne seemed to find it so difficult to manage a household. He didn't appreciate her reluctance to oversee servants, a constant problem when she was unwilling to do things herself, and totally uninterested in housework. She was not immune to criticism, being depressed when Tommy, after a visit to Scotland where his hostess, 'a wonderful housekeeper', had organized tea for a huge gathering, complained that their own 'house was a shambles'. But domestic matters were never a priority for her. It was Tommy, Tessa pointed out, who did the washing up. When Tessa was despatched to boarding school, rather abruptly at the age of thirteen, it was Tommy who sewed on the nametapes.

Right from the beginning of her married life, she had needed support. The role of housewife did not come naturally to her. Not long after she had settled in Cannon Hall Cottage, she wrote to Gladys Cooper, a long-standing friend of the family, in some desperation asking for help in locating a cook. Gladys came to the rescue, suggesting Lily Bocock, one of her own former staff. Lily remained for some years, though she soon met and married George Richards, Tommy's soldier-servant. He left the army in 1934 but he and Lily stayed with Brownings until they went to Egypt in 1936. (They had a daughter whom they named Tessa too, as Daphne's daughter Tessa later discovered.)

The arrival of children meant that nanny and nursemaids were necessary for Daphne so that she could concentrate on her work. It was not until Christian was born that she concerned herself much at all with childcare. Then – to the surprise of all about her – she insisted on attending to his needs. Even so, she was rather shocked by the reality of having to tend him on her own. When she was left in sole charge of Christian, the girls having gone with their nanny, Margaret, to stay with Granny Browning – she was not enthused. Motherhood did not come naturally to her, she complained to Tod: '6am never has been and never will be my finest hour, whatever Winston Churchill might say. To be leapt upon and scratched by a lusty youngster of ten months shouting at the top of his voice may delight the tender hearts of a J.M. Barrie mother, but I feel a factory may be more soothing.'

Apart from looking after the children, Margaret could also cook, which was a distinct advantage to begin with at Readymoney and later at Menabilly. But Margaret had her hands full with the three children, and Daphne soon employed Mrs Staton, who would arrive in time to prepare and take Daphne her breakfast in bed. That arrangement, however, did not last long. In February 1943, when Daphne had rushed to Netheravon in Wiltshire to be with Tommy after a glider accident, she heard that all was not well at Readymoney:

I return to Fowey on Monday to domestic chaos. The new cook, an ex-nurse friend of Margaret's apparently having had a flare up with Margaret in my absence. Aren't they a hopeless lot! You would think everyone would be as tactful as possible in these days of servant difficulties. Margaret is very loyal, but she is used to ruling the roost. I can foresee a summer of nursery-maiding ahead of me, with cooking thrown in! What a life. Anyway the daffodils will soon be in bloom, and I always feel more cheerful when spring is on the way.

And soon she had organized a very satisfactory replacement. Fortunately for her, Mrs Hancock, a sister-in-law of George Hunkin, who had been their cook at Greyfriars in 1937, had retired and returned to Fowey, so she came in to do much of the cooking.

Margaret was also a skilful seamstress, and made all the children's clothes, including beautifully smocked dresses. But from an early stage, she was afflicted with periods of illness, including migraines, when she would lie in a darkened room for up to a week at a time and Daphne would have to take over. These periods of incapacity caused an undercurrent of anxiety. When Daphne obtained the lease for Menabilly, amid all the huge obstacles that were put in her way the potential problem that concerned her most was whether Margaret's health would hold out during the move. Daphne tried many solutions – despatching her to different doctors, sending her on holidays, giving her a break from cooking by asking 'nice Mrs Hancock to come and hold the fort' – but none had any lasting effect. Margaret left Menabilly in 1945. Daphne gave her money to set herself up in business making children's clothes, as she was so expert at that, though in the end she took up a post with another family.

Daphne often paid attention to the needs and feelings of her employees – as when she moved from Greyfriars to Hythe, to the Commandant's House, rather reluctantly: one compensation was that she thought 'staff' would much prefer Hythe to the 'wastes of Salisbury Plain'. Life as an army wife should have had its compensations, staffwise, especially perhaps in Egypt, where there was no shortage of domestic help (Tessa, who was then barely three, remembers the cook who prayed towards Mecca five times a day), but Hassan the housekeeper expected to be given orders, which only underlined the feelings of inadequacy that dogged Daphne in that period. Tommy was much better able to cope with his soldier-servants – George Richards, and then Johnson, his replacement, who looked after Daphne's interests too. When Tessa and Flavia were staying at Margaret's cottage, it was Johnson who drove Daphne down to see them (when, according to Flavia, 'we would set up a howl and cling to her skirts', much to the upset of Margaret). It was Johnson who found the billet at Langley End, Daphne's home for part of the war. When he was demobilized in 1945, Tommy wrote to Daphne to ask: did she intend having a manservant at Menabilly? That was a telling way of putting it, acknowledging that Daphne was in charge of the household there. She obviously felt in something of a quandary, but she didn't want Johnson there without Tommy – and Tommy was not to return to England until 1946, and, in fact, did not then live at Menabilly full-time.

The war years were inevitably topsy-turvy. A succinct sign of social status even in those straitened times, however, was the fact that when she moved into Langley End as a paying guest, she took her housemaid with her. And when she and the children were invited back to Langley End after Kits's birth, it was with three members of staff as well as the three children: nanny, nursemaid and housemaid. But only Margaret moved with the family to Readymoney: the nursemaid Prim, fondly remembered by Flavia, had to leave, as there was no room for any live-in staff, apart from Margaret. The cook, whether Mrs Staton or Mrs Hancock, lived locally, as did 'two minions' who came in to do the cleaning.

This was the beginning of the rather more pared-down staff that reflected the shift nationally after the war.

Menabilly presented particular problems, remote – and chilly – as it was. The vastness of the rooms with their high ceilings meant that there was a continual battle to combat the bitter cold – much feeding of the fires, much fetching and carrying of logs, and some of it even done by Daphne. As she said rather ruefully in one of her asides about the household, 'everything seems so much easier in the summer.' And though they were renting the house, not the estate, there was the need to keep the grounds close to the house in order too. Mr Burt (whom Kits nicknamed 'Dang Me', as this was his usual expression) from the nearby hamlet of Hamelin helped out: chopping branches, mowing the lawn for Kits to play cricket, bringing coal in.

Daphne hired two very young sisters to help in the house: Violet and Joyce, who shared a bedroom there. Their work was supplemented by daily help provided by Margaret, who lived on the estate (and who initially thought that Daphne must be a guest, as she was so retiring). This went well until Daphne reported to Tod that 'the mainstay of our staff after Nanny, a little red-haired girl, is having a baby in July' and shortly afterwards that 'the little daily help has departed to a cafe (the bright lights of Fowey)'. They were left with the services of a fourteen-year-old: 'All right in the summer, but I view the autumn and fires with misgiving.'

However, Joyce was soon back: Daphne related in a very matter-of-fact way that Joyce had had a baby girl, and a home had been found for her. But it was a continual jigsaw of coping with departures and arrivals, and needing constantly to give instructions or sort out arguments. There were different cooks stepping in when Nanny took to her bed for days at a time: Mrs Hancock, Mrs Burt (who was popular with the children, as she was homely and cheerful), and eventually Gladys Powell, remembered affectionately by the children, who came in 1948 and stayed ten years. Joyce cooked too, as did Violet, who became

DAPHNE DU MAURIER AT HOME

rather keen on looking up new recipes: Daphne writes of Violet and Tessa concocting tasty things in the kitchen.

At one point, when there was again 'trouble with Joyce', this time because she was getting married, Daphne mused on possible solutions. What to do? Whether to make do with current arrangements, perhaps supplemented by 'caravan-help and local try-outs or to try for foreigners'. Tommy was in favour of finding a foreign couple. 'But how does one set about it? I am told Italians are now much the best.' They did everything, she understood, from driving to pressing one's clothes 'but have *bambini* every year'.

She was sceptical of finding the 'dream couple'. 'The trouble with a really good couple is the snags and drawbacks of the house itself and odd things like fetching the milk, fetching the papers, all the breakfast trays and odds and ends that we all take for granted, but "superior" types might object to. The place is so very off the map too.'

It was all rather different from the Menabilly of her fiction – Manderley with the huge staff that so intimidated the second Mrs de Winter, quite apart from the housekeeper: Mrs Danvers, who dominates the action in the book in magnificently sinister style, perhaps represents the worst of Daphne's fears over servants. Mrs Danvers is not untypical, in that many of the servants in Daphne's books are characters, not part of the convenient background: Matty, the loyal and resourceful maid, and companion, of Honor Harris in *The King's General*; William, the similarly inventive

manservant in charge of Navron in *Frenchman's Creek*; old Seecombe, the steward supervising the solely male staff in the household of *My Cousin Rachel*.

One development that made things run more smoothly at Menabilly was the arrival of Tod, who became a crucial member of the household. She had remained Daphne's valued friend and confidante after the three years she had spent at Cannon Hall as a governess (and stuck firmly to calling her Daphne, despite the family habit of nicknames: Daphne was Bing, Track or Tray). Soon after moving to Menabilly Daphne invited Tod, who was acting as a companion to an elderly couple in Yorkshire, to stay for a holiday – offering a surprising attraction: 'We might even let the "cataract cook" have a long weekend off, and cope with the cooking ourselves, the 16-year-olds assisting.' Whether it was the self-catering or not, the visit was so successful that Daphne began to machinate about Tod coming to live at Menabilly permanently to take over the education of the children. She sent her a twelve-page letter laying out 'tremendous mad schemes of post-war plans and you coming down to "gov" the children'. Daphne was 'so delighted the children took to you so much' and enticed her with the prospect of being 'enthroned' in the 'charming room' overlooking the lawn. Tessa could change her bedroom: Daphne could see the 'room beyond that with all the cupboards as a cosy little schoolroom', and she underlined the inducement that 'you could bring all your own furniture from store'. However, realistically, Daphne could also see the advantages of Tod staying at her current post in Yorkshire: 'There is something about a houseful of servants and central heating that is by no means to be despised in these days.'

Later, there was a suggestion of Tod taking over the self-contained flat at Menabilly, though at that point it was the temporary home of Marjorie Johnson, the wife of Tommy's new soldier-servant. And, before any agreement could be made, there must be consideration of what Tommy would think. 'The idea

Tod, Daphne's governess for three years and then a close friend, is seen here, with Flavia and Kits, after Daphne enticed her to Menabilly to educate her children.

of a "resident gov" has always been his nightmare too – making hearty conversation at meals etc, but I feel everything would be on such a different footing with you and one could say what one likes . . .' (This, in fact, proved not to be the case.)

But the following year another solution presented itself, when a Miss Riley, living conveniently nearby in St Austell, approached Daphne and offered to be a daily governess, as Daphne explained as diplomatically as possible in a twenty-page letter to Tod. However, when Daphne offered Miss Riley the job, she informed Tod in her next – short – letter, 'the paragon' turned it down for a better offer, rather to Daphne's chagrin, though she added to Tod: 'Looking forward to a good laugh over this, and talks upon the future when you come.'

When Daphne solicited Tod's help again, this time it was accepted, as her employer had died. There ensued careful negotiation about terms and conditions. Daphne was very used now to being on her own, and laid out her desire for solitude: she had 'this awful, rather selfish thing' about the evenings with a 'curious little winter routine of a tray by the fire, and I sit and read or write my letters and it is complete relaxation.'

But, anxious to make everything comfortable for Tod, she went shopping, reporting back details about how the now-vacant flat was being prepared, including staining floorboards at the edge in case the carpet wasn't big enough, installing new lino for the bathroom and kitchen, and listing things she had bought, including 'comfy armchairs and bureau-cum-bookcase', but also instructing Tod to go into York and buy what she wanted. Daphne was, as ever, generous.

And so Tod came back into Daphne's household as a governess to her children. She also took over much of the management of the house, and a little bit of the gardening: she had her own garden at the side of the house, growing salads and flowers for the house, such as pinks, gladioli, night-scented stock, and sweet peas among the raspberries. Her other great pastime was painting watercolours, something that on occasion she shared with Flavia.

Life became much easier for Daphne in most respects, as she could rely on her loyal friend to supervise the children – and the home. For when the need for her as a governess ended, she stayed on as *de facto* manager. Tod occupied a curious position, partly employee and partly friend. 'They would not sit down and have tea together,' said Flavia. 'Tod would be up in her flat.' Though she often cooked for herself in her flat – the children particularly enjoyed visiting her there and sampling her cake – she would also eat sometimes with the family. That could be awkward when Tommy was there, as they did not get on well; Daphne would frequently be thrust into the position of peacemaker.

That was a position that Daphne often occupied in respect of the household too, as Tod had a tendency to be rivalrous: 'She and Mr Burt were always falling out,' said Flavia. Though Daphne had people to help with the house, she was faced with that conundrum of managing the people who managed the house, as she vented in a letter to Oriel: 'Oh hell, Tod keeps coming to interrupt about the food for the weekend, and that Gladys is being disobliging, and that Mr Burt has had too much tea at eleven – I shall go dotty!'

There were too the mysteries of National Insurance to consider. In 1959 there was a series of letters about this nuisance aspect of housekeeping. 'The damn Insurance man has been round here snooping.' There were problems with Mr Burt's card – 'It seems as if I should have been paying 8/3 for him for YEARS and Dang Me himself 8d' – and the discovery that Tod had to have a card too, although she was over sixty-five: 'the long and the short of it is that persons over 65 up to 90 or 100, it doesn't matter, still have to have a card for National Insurance.'

By the end of the 1950s, the household had changed. Both Tessa and Flavia were married. Tommy was living full time in Menabilly – which for the sake of harmony meant that Tod could

Esther Rowe, who lived in a cottage on the Menabilly estate, was persuaded by Tod to help out temporarily in 1958 and then stayed for thirty years as housekeeper.

Menabilly during the war) lived with her husband, Henry, and young son, Ralph, in a cottage on the Menabilly estate, just on the other side of the big lawn and behind the belt of trees. She was looking for secretarial work, and had applied to the estate agent May Whetter and Grose in Par. One day in 1958 Tod came to see her in some desperation because Gladys, the cook, was expecting a baby, and short-term help was needed. At first Esther refused, but when Tod returned to ask again, she agreed to give it a try temporarily. Gladys's baby turned out to be twins, and Esther stayed. When she was offered the secretarial job, she turned it down.

Convenient as it was, just across the lawn, she found the part-time post quite congenial. Her morning routine was straightforward: 'In the morning I would open all the shutters, fill all the oil heaters, light the fire, make the beds and put Daphne's breakfast on a tray: Ryvita with honey comb, and a cafetière of coffee. I would take it up to her, saying "Good Morning Lady Browning."'

There was no conversation between them, and her efforts were taken for granted, even with the morning breakfast tray. 'But she never interfered with your work. She would be in the hut by 11, and after making lunch – something simple: a little fillet steak, fish, chicken – I would be gone. I'd see her and the General going out with their little dogs for their walk up to the Gribbin, such long strides. They were an elegant couple.'

She found them easy to work for, especially Tommy, who

not. But as Kits was now living at Whitelands House in London, the solution was that she would go there and cook for him. One of Tod's last acts at Menabilly was to find someone else who would ease Daphne's life – as it turned out, for the rest of her life. Esther Rowe (the sister-in-law of Margaret, who had worked briefly at

Tod's watercolour of Menabilly, with its famous rhododendrons in the foreground.

was cheered by having someone young and lively about the house. And she appreciated his sense of humour: 'One day I was cleaning the floor, and I began to scrub the steps at the side when the General came in and said, "For goodness sake, the days of slavery have gone".' She also remembers Tommy's kindness: 'The General gave us his old Ford, the car he used in Egypt.' And he offered them a stay in the flat in Whitelands House. 'My husband took us up in the car. We had a week's holiday there: we thought we were made!' This was a rarity. She did not often have time off when she worked for Daphne. 'I did go on jury service once, and the case finished on the first day but I took the second day too!'

There was, however, the occasional touch of glamour, such as the Queen's visit in 1962. Esther remembers that day well, because she entertained the entourage of chauffeurs and detectives at her house: she laid on a grand tea in her dining room, with pasties, sausage rolls, trifles and splits. 'My God,' said Tommy, when he happened to see it, 'you've got better food than us.' They were eating delicate salmon and cucumber sandwiches cut into triangles, supplied by a caterer in St Austell.

Esther quickly became a mainstay of the household, and

after Tommy's death she was invaluable. Though Daphne, undemonstrative as ever, may not have said as much to Esther, she began to depend on her, as is plain from her letters: 'Solid getting on with a working routine is much easier alone (but of course, I would be done without Esther doing the lunch!).' When the plan to move to Kilmarth finally came to fruition, Daphne asked if she and Henry would move with her. In principle, they agreed, but they didn't like the flat at Kilmarth that was at first offered. Daphne promptly offered to convert the stable block there into a three-bedroom cottage for them. It would 'cost an awful lot. But I must do it, as I never could live there without them.' Later she wrote to Oriel, 'I have prepared Esther, and she and Henry are thrilled at the thought of a new home designed for their comfort, so that is one great relief. So ghastly if they had said, "We are so sorry, but we really feel we had rather stay here and look after the Rashleighs."'

Sadly, Esther's move to the smart new conversion at Kilmarth was without Henry, as he died suddenly from hepatitis in October 1968. It was during the following year, when Daphne was trying to tempt Esther out of her sadness, that she lent the fur coat: 'Last week, I made her go to a dance in Newquay, and she wore my best fur coat and stayed the night in Newquay, and I think it cheered her up. Today she has gone off to look at a kitchen unit for her new cottage. But it *must* be sad having to plan without Henry.'

Daphne was encouraged by her seeming better, and was hopeful for her social life, writing 'she is always rushing off looking smart with earrings'. Esther did find a new partner, Denis Drew, a teacher, who also provided part of the support by collecting logs. Daphne called him 'the Percy Thrower of Kilmarth', because he looked after the plants in her porch. He proudly claims that Daphne actually used the pair of egg coddlers he bought her – a rare burst of domestic activity on her part (though he also pointed out that she used to make sloe gin with Tommy).

Esther was rather put out to find, much later, that Daphne had grumbled to Foy Quiller-Couch when Esther was going to a hunt ball that times had certainly changed if *anyone* could go now. But on the whole the domestic arrangements suited them both. After the move to Kilmarth Esther became indispensable. She knew how necessary Daphne's 'routes' were – from breakfast in bed to the ringing of the lunchtime gong – and how important it was that things were just as they used to be, which was not always easy: when Daphne asked Esther to buy her a suitcase, she couldn't deal with the new-fangled combination locks, demanding one with a key.

Esther could even put her secretarial training into practice, at last, as she helped Daphne answer letters, kept tabs on bills and dealt with administration, as well as keeping control of fans, who found their way to Daphne's door. In the last few years, she was in charge of organizing the rota of nurses and companions. Jennette Martin was one of those companions, living in from Friday evening to Monday morning. 'There were several nurses and companions, but we never met each other. Esther had everything timed to a T. I would take out my bedding from the chest of drawers in the hall, which had names on: that's how I knew there were other people.'

For Daphne, Esther's loyalty solved the problem of managing a household. It was something which she had had to deal with unwillingly all her life, and solving it was necessary to free her up so that she was able to live the life of her imagination. She needed solitude, but to achieve solitude she had to have staff. The difficulties that the second Mrs de Winter so famously had with her inability to manage servants at Manderley were a reflection of Daphne's own reluctance to supervise them. For the last part of her life, Daphne could rely on Esther to deal with all that. And for Daphne, in an increasingly uncertain world, Esther provided a thread of continuity. As Esther said: 'She was used to me. And I was used to her.'

CHAPTER 8
KILMARTH: 'THE LAST FRONTIER'

Despite her inclination for solitude, widowhood had taken Daphne by surprise. She missed Tommy's company and his humour. For a while, as she wrote in an essay on death and widowhood, she wore his shirts, sat at his writing desk, used his pen and continued their evening rituals. She wore black and white for a year.

But in the midst of her grief for Tommy, she felt that a burden had been lifted from her: 'What I didn't realise is that for years I had been living under a strain of angst about his health (whether physical or mental), and although when he was OK I was perfectly happy, there was an underlying worry.' She was now feeling 'a sort of contentment'.

And she had the faintest 'brew' of an idea – of an invasion of Britain, and how it would affect a place like Fowey. 'Who would collaborate, and who would be Resistance? The title is possibly *The Take-over Bid*. It's only a faint seed, but I do see the possibilities of an exciting story in this. It could be satirical as well – showing up the sort of people who are with the invaders and who are not.' In fact, that seed did not germinate for five years.

Daphne at the writing desk in the Long Room at Menabilly (with its statuette of Gerald), which went with her to Kilmarth.

It remained a comfort to her that Tommy had seen and approved of Kilmarth, and had signed the lease for it. In the summer of 1964, she and Tessa had inspected Kilmarth, the eighteenth-century dower house of Menabilly, and found it 'much nicer than I had expected, and as a second string to Mena, very good indeed'. The site was 'superb, the most glorious view of the bay, and the house itself, though not large and gracious and lovely like Mena, has a definite charm'. Its exposed location was as different as could be to the sheltered isolation of Menabilly, as it was situated on a clifftop, with its large front garden behind railings at the top of the lane leading down to the village of Polkerris and the Rashleigh Inn. It seemed, by comparison, to be in full view of the world. It was, however, a comfortable and attractive house (Kits preferred it to Menabilly) and she liked the fact that the foundations of the house were fourteenth century, and that 'Kilmarth' meant 'retreat of King Mark': she thought of it later as a last frontier.

But Daphne was then still living, heart and soul, in the house she felt so at one with, savouring the time remaining to her at Menabilly. Kilmarth was a back-up; it was not what she wanted for her future. Then in 1965, with four years of her lease still to run, Philip Rashleigh suggested that, as Kilmarth was empty now after the death of its tenant, she could move there imminently, so that the Rashleighs could repossess Menabilly. Negotiations were on again. By the end of July 1965 it seemed to Daphne that Philip had agreed to her staying at Menabilly for another fifteen years, until 1980, with the promise that she could build her own dower house thereafter in the grounds of Menabilly, in return for which she would relinquish Kilmarth and pay for the demolition of the unused wing of Menabilly, if it did not exceed £5,000. She allowed herself to relax. 'I did not want to leave Mena. It's my home, and my routes.'

She began to adjust to life alone. There were holidays with her family – she enjoyed two Hellenic cruises with Tessa, and became friendly with the vice-chancellor of Reading University, Sir John Wolfenden, who was one of the guest lecturers. She bought a car, a bright red DAF, 'a dear little thing', in which, after driving it about the paths at Menabilly to get back into practice, she passed her test and took to buzzing about the lanes at high speed: her grandchildren called her the Niki Lauda of Cornwall. She even took herself off, rather intrepidly, to visit Jeanne on Dartmoor. She had appreciated the need for more independence – and a car would, anyway, be handy for visiting a cousin of her mother's, Dora, a woman of ninety who had suddenly decided to come and live in Tywardreath. Not long afterwards, Daphne's elderly aunt Billie came to live nearby. Daphne added these two to the rota of other elderly neighbours she visited.

In January 1966, the spectre of departure arose again. Philip was wobbling; he hadn't agreed an extension after all. There followed another two agonizing weeks of suspense, after which he decided finally that he would not grant the fifteen-year lease; nor did he want Daphne to build a house in the grounds. He seemed absolutely determined. The only option was Kilmarth. She hoped to buy it, but that was refused as well. And yet, and yet . . . still nothing seemed to be quite finally settled. For someone who liked to be sure of her routine, it must have been a very nerve-racking time.

ABOVE Tommy's MG, photographed here by Tommy. Though Daphne had learned to drive when she was young, she never drove after her marriage. After Tommy's death she bought a DAF, with automatic transmission, and passed her driving test.
RIGHT Daphne at work on her Adler typewriter at Kilmarth.

But like the true professional she was, Daphne carried on with the research for her new book, which she had been mulling over at Christmas. She had been trying to jump-start her fiction again. She had taken a trip to Venice in the autumn with Jeanne in the hope of finding inspiration for a story. It hadn't worked – or at least, not just then: in 1970, a 'very brilliant and interesting talk about Great Intellectual Thoughts' with author and friend Colin Wilson spurred her on to write some short stories, including 'Don't Look Now', set horribly atmospherically in Venice. (The film *Don't Look Now* was made in 1973, and met with Daphne's unqualified approval – though she was shown a version without the sex scene.) But now she had a new project, as she had rather gleefully told Oriel. It would be 'one of those rather irritating

books that are in fashion nowadays – they are called "coffee table books", and they cost about three guineas, and people have them displayed as a status symbol. No-one ever reads them! Well, I suddenly thought I might jump on the bandwagon and do one called *Romantic Cornwall,* and get Kits to do heaps of coloured photographs.'

In the end the book was called *Vanishing Cornwall* – 'Romantic Cornwall' had been her American publisher's suggestion but she hated the word 'romantic', and, anyway, the concept of 'vanishing' fitted in much more with her rather pessimistic outlook on the culture of Cornwall. She was scathing about tourism. In a letter about this time to the writer Leo Walmsley, she wrote: 'I get spasms all over when I walk down to Pridmouth, hoping for a quiet swim and find hordes of people playing transistors'; she feared that an influx of visitors would turn Cornwall into 'the playground of all England'.

Though she was cynical about 'coffee table books', she was earnest about her commission about her adopted home. It was a chance to write a manifesto:

> A country known and loved in all its moods becomes woven into the pattern of life, something to be shared, to be made plain. Those born and bred in Cornwall must have the greatest understanding of its people and their ways, its history and its legends, its potentiality for future growth. As one who sought to know it long ago, at five years old, in quest of freedom, and later put down roots and found content, I have come a small way on the path. The beauty and the mystery beckon still.

Her investigation of 'the spirit of Cornwall' took her mind off Menabilly and took her on pleasurable excursions with Kits. Their reconnaissance trips along coasts and over moors, taking in ruined engine houses and the extraordinary tale of the Vicar

ABOVE Harrington Mann's portrait of Daphne when she was fifteen remained a favourite of hers throughout her life.
RIGHT The interconnecting rooms at Kilmarth, with the doors open, reminded Daphne of the Long Room at Menabilly, and so were given the same name.

of Warleggan, who preached to a congregation of cardboard cut-outs, were undertaken in March. 'We went round in the early spring, as she didn't want Cornwall to be full of trippers,' said Kits, for whom it was a 'magical' three weeks. In the evening they would sit by the fire, Daphne with her whisky and Kits with his beer, 'and she would brief me about the next day's expedition, the places to be visited and the various strange characters that had inhabited them.' There was, he added, a lot of giggling.

She dedicated *Vanishing Cornwall* 'to the memory of my husband, because of memories shared and a mutual love for Cornwall; and to our son Christian, who photographed the present, while I rambled on about the past'.

It was published in 1967 – the year she joined Mebyon Kernow,

the Cornish nationalist party, and the year Philip Rashleigh finally made up his mind. He did want to move down; he did not want to renew her lease. This time he came to speak to Daphne himself, rather than conducting the affair through his agent and lawyers, as had been the case previously. He was, she said, so clearly in such a state about it that she was very gracious to him, entertaining him and his mother by the fireside of her precious Long Room.

The move to Kilmarth was at last inevitable. At least, she thought, she had saved money on pulling down the disused wing, and could use the money saved for a cottage for Esther just next door: she would be alone in the house (unlike an earlier resident, William Rashleigh, 'landed proprietor', who in 1850 had a butler and six other live-in servants). She began to think seriously about

the move. Much needed to be done, as the previous tenants had neglected the house. 'It's costing the earth,' she told A.L. Rowse.

She was, reluctantly, becoming reconciled to her new home. In one of her visits there she had met the farmer who would be her tenant and who was going to cut the grass and weeds round about the house. She wrote to Oriel, 'I'm beginning to be rather *torn* between both places. It would be fun to have both, and to move between the two houses, as my whims increase with my old age!' And with a note of determination she said later, 'I *know* I can make the house cheerful and welcoming.'

One thing was certain: Kilmarth would be more manageable.

Though Daphne remained utterly committed to Menabilly, it has to be remembered that others did not always view it in the same light as she did. When A.L. Rowse visited her before she moved, he found a rather desolate landscape: 'I hadn't been along the Rashleigh country for years. Here were the gates, one of the fine pillars crashed into by a lorry and left unsafe, the lodge empty, stinging nettles grown up in the yard, The park landscape beautiful as ever, but fallen trunks uncleared away.'

He was struck too by the shabbiness of the interior, adding in his inimitably superior style: 'What surprised me was that Daphne was no aesthete, had not much taste. It was a family house, lived

LEFT Daphne enjoyed the garden at Kilmarth, though she had no interest in horticulture: she would have marvelled that, under its current owner, it won the most trophies at the 2011 Cornwall Garden Society show.

BELOW *Ygdrasil* came with Daphne from Menabilly, and found her last resting place under the trees, where Daphne's grandchildren played on her.

the chic of Easton Neston or Evangeline Bruce's embassy. Daphne was where she always had been: a bourgeois background. It was I who had moved on.'

Still, he was willing to give her the benefit of his wisdom over tea in the Long Room. They talked about her writing block. 'She had two or three ideas for short stories, but even these wouldn't "gel" (horrid word). She couldn't write unless the whole thing came clear in her head and possessed her.' Feeling sorry for her, Rowse made suggestions for subjects, such as a biography of her husband, and was rather put out when she turned that down. He then gave her a list of some suitable reading, including Tolstoy's short stories and Kipling's 'The Gardener'. 'She hadn't read any of them, living so solitary, so unintellectual a life, not really educated. This is part of the trouble, I suspect: she has nobody to tell her, no pace-makers, nobody to correct her style.'

This arrogance is entirely in keeping with Rowse's character; what is more surprising is that he toyed with ideas of seduction as she showed him over Menabilly for the last time, including the bedrooms. 'But it would have been a mistake, no passions roused. We went quickly through the General's room – a boy's room: full of caps and cups and racquets and odds and ends of sports and tackle – like the bedroom of a school prefect or captain of boats at a university. "I hadn't the heart to touch it," she said. How would it be if she married someone sophisticated, more complex, less of a boy, and more of a man? She might get a new lease of inspiration. But she is a solitary; and so am I, too old to turn over a new leaf and make new adjustments now.'

in, fine rooms devoted to play-rooms, the untidiness of having children about the house. That is what the money has gone into – no furniture worth noticing, worn carpets, toys, TV, radio games.' He would have done differently, he said; he would have made it 'a treasurehouse'. 'Daphne had it comfortable and shabby. It revealed her – interested only in writing.'

As Daphne showed him all over the house, Rowse noted disparagingly that 'even the double guest-room had nothing much in the way of furniture' and continually contrasted it with other houses with which he was name-droppingly familiar: 'The Johnstones' Trewithen, Helen Mildmay's Mothecombe, let alone

But he concluded that she certainly needed 'more intelligent society', and he selflessly made himself available for that. 'It was obvious she wanted a heart to heart talk, and we had it. I said that Kilmarth, if she should have to move, might prove another inspiration, another phase. She was aware of that, but didn't want to leave – she looked at the place that is her life, has become a fixation, so that she doesn't mind inhabiting it entirely alone. As an old lady of seventy she wouldn't mind going further up the road, but not yet.'

Rowse was right about Kilmarth providing inspiration. A dwelling on that spot had existed since 1327, and on one of her visits Daphne found in the cellars the remains of experiments by the previous tenant, a Professor Singer; there were glass jars containing biological specimens such as embryos of animals. She learned more of its original inhabitant, Roger Kylmerth. And before long she had hatched the plot for *The House on the Strand*, a novel that dips back and forth between the fourteenth century and the present, as her narrator, Dick, took an experimental drug that could transport him directly to the past. It would encompass many of her interests – history, psychology, biochemistry and theories of dreams – as Dick flees as often as he can to the past, which he prefers: 'I remembered how I had walked about that other world with a dreamer's freedom but with a waking man's perception.'

But, as usual, she needed the facts. She threw herself into research into Cornwall in the fourteenth century and the way the bay had changed, getting, blissfully, 'rather brewified about Kilmarth in olden days'. She read intensively about Tywardreath Priory, which was developing as a focal point for her new plot. ('Tywardreath' means 'the house on the strand'.) She pondered on the Singers, and on alchemy: 'So I thought – what if they found some secret way of going back to the past? And suddenly I began to see the whole countryside in a fourteenth-century way, and the sea roaring up past Par . . .'

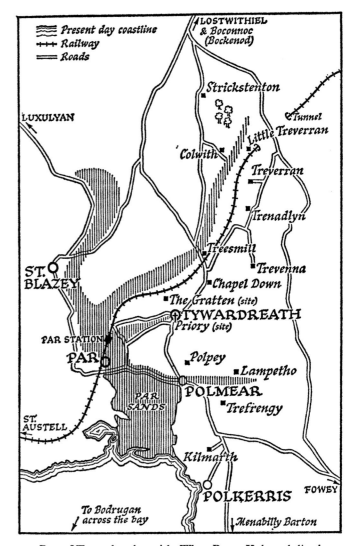

Part of Tywardreath parish. When Roger Kylmerth lived, the shaded area was estuary.

ABOVE The frontispiece map of *The House on the Strand* drew on Daphne's extensive walks around the countryside.
RIGHT Daphne was particularly fond of checked shirts and had a large collection of leather belts.

She walked the landscape, trying to judge the exact position of long-dead houses, tracking over the fields to try to find the sites of old villages. She was going round all the old farms in the district,

'with field glasses, and I am sure people think that I am a spy, hovering about in hedges!' It was all 'rather fun' and reminded her of games she had played on Hampstead Heath.

She spent a lot of time studying an old tithe map and filling in the names of all the fields; she was full of glee when one turned out to be called 'Bishop's Down' or 'Prior's Meadow'. 'You think "Aha, this was part of their land!" Useless information perhaps, but not to me, seeing an old Bishop in his litter travelling down across-country from Exeter to Tywardreath, to admonish the Prior!' She took advice from her GP, Dr Luther, about the physical effects of mind-altering drugs (inscribing a copy of the final published book 'For Martin, my collaborator but for whom I might have had even wilder theories than are put forward in this book'). The encounter in a lay-by between Dick and Dr Powell was based on an actual event. The walking stick with a flask in the stem

existed: Dr Luther's daughter Mary, a regular visitor at Menabilly and Kilmarth and now curator of Fowey Museum, said that there had been one just like it in the hall at Menabilly.

The reader could have the book in one hand (with its frontispiece map of the area) and a modern map in the other, and perfectly follow the landmarks from Kilmarth to the almshouses at the base of Polmear Hill, past the church and churchyard, and to the villages around. This is the one time that her long-standing editor Sheila Hodges visited her, and they tramped the scenery together to see if the topography of the book stood up:

Each morning the two of us – Daphne dressed, as usual, in her elegant but well-worn trousers and sweater, a stout walking-stick in her hand – would tramp every inch of the terrain which Dick, under the influence of the drug,

The wind-bent trees around Kilmarth, in its much more exposed spot, fascinated Daphne, reminding her of those in Arthur Rackham's drawings.

had covered six centuries before. It was a fascinating and revelatory experience . . . Daphne became Dick; I ceased to exist for her. Through her eyes I saw a fourteenth-century otter hunt in a spinney at the foot of a hill, and together we scrambled across the railway line just as Dick had done in his journeys between the past and the present, when, lost in the fourteenth century, he all but plunged beneath the wheels of a twentieth-century train.

Writing the book was exhilarating and an enormous boon for her, taking her mind off her real-life problems. But she admitted to getting tired more quickly. She still worked quite a full day, from 11.00 a.m. to 1.00 p.m., and from 2.00 to 3.30 p.m. Then she would take a walk, after which she would work from 5.30 to 7.30 p.m. 'I am quite exhausted, and glad to have my sups with the "telly", at which I sometimes fall asleep.'

The House on the Strand, with its dedication 'for my predecessors at Kilmarth', was published in 1969, the year that she finally moved. Yet again, in a curious way, fact was following fiction,

DAPHNE DU MAURIER AT HOME

as she was moving into the house she had written about, just as she had moved into Menabilly after creating Manderley. But this time the process was rather more drawn out. Preparations had been going on for a long time. In her article 'Moving House', she wrote of how she would 'visit the empty house, walk round the rooms, plan the decorations, watch the necessary alterations, decide where the furniture would ultimately go. The architect, the builder, the builder's craftsmen could not have been more helpful or more kind. We felt ourselves a team, creating a renewed Kilmarth, which I felt very certain its predecessors had loved.'

This was no doubt true – Kits spoke highly of Mr Pascoe the builder, who was 'absolutely wonderful' – but it conveys a sense of calm and positive resignation that perhaps belies the great effort that had gone into making the transition as painless as possible, with everything made as similar to Menabilly as possible: 'He moved her room by room,' said Kits. 'There would be the same colour carpet, curtains, furniture; all the contents of one room would be moved at a time.' The 'James Barrie chair' – the one the author had sat in as he watched the du Maurier children playing Peter Pan – was placed in the main sitting room. Tommy's bows and arrows, and walking sticks, were in the inner hall, just as at Menabilly. In a television interview with Wilfred De'ath for the BBC in 1971 – which was the first time she had agreed to be filmed (and the film can still be seen online in the BBC Archive) – she greeted him in the hall, saying, 'I tried to get it as much like Menabilly as possible,' indicating sticks, bows and arrows and portraits.

Family and friends were giving advice and assistance. Tod came back from London: 'Tod was on the go non-stop, with carting plants backwards and forwards to Kilmarth, and she really *is* amazing at eighty – her *energy*!' Flavia and Tessa chose carpets and furnishings, though some from Cannon Hall days, like the curtains, remained. 'Everything always looked nice,' said Flavia, 'but she wasn't interested really.' Typically, Daphne insisted on

keeping her own room shabby and familiar, but she did revel in a little extra luxury: 'I have never before had a suite of dressing room, bathroom and bedroom.'

She spent her last Christmas at Menabilly, piquantly, on her own: 'It's so queer having no one down here.' It had been a bleak few weeks, when Kits's sons had been in a car accident, and Esther's husband had died suddenly. But any sadness was ameliorated by the men orbiting round the moon, the 'most exciting thing that has happened, historically, for generations. I keep dashing to the telly, to see what has happened.'

She took last walks along the paths she knew so well, and experienced feelings of melancholy as she sat in the Long Room 'with awful echoes all round me'. Her archive was transported to one of the stone basement rooms at Kilmarth, the old kitchen, and 'every day I clear out more drawers and more cupboards', she wrote wearily to Oriel, reporting that 'Little Arthur has gone (the furniture I mean), and is all installed in the Pink Room, with its pink bathroom, at Kilmarth (your room); and so it goes on bit by bit. Which really does help, because by getting myself denuded here, it's like a baby being weaned.'

She made the final step in June 1969, the same month that she was created a dame in the Birthday Honours list. Though she accepted the honour – and reluctantly attended the investiture – she did not use the title. Still, it was perhaps a distraction from the heartache of leaving Menabilly – a feeling shared by Flavia: 'Leaving Menabilly for the last time was agony. I adored it. It was really magic. I dream of it sometimes now.'

Daphne could see the consolations of Kilmarth. She loved the view, 'the best I have ever known', especially from her bedroom, which had windows on two sides, and she could watch the ships anchored out at sea before entering Par harbour. She was very struck by the trees, twisted into shapes by the wind on the exposed position – trees like those in Arthur Rackham's drawings, she said. She appreciated the feel of the house, which was quite

ABOVE Daphne was very proud of her new kitchen at Kilmarth, which was full of modern appliances – though she still had no interest in actually using them.
RIGHT Tommy's array of arrows, which had been displayed at Menabilly, were carefully transferred to Kilmarth.

different from Menabilly's: there was so much sun. The drawing room, dining room and library opened into each other, echoing the Long Room at Menabilly, and were therefore given that name. When the doors of all three were opened, one could see from one end of the house to the other, which gave a sense of space. And, on a bright day, sun flooded through. In the winter she revelled in the night storage heaters, which made the house snug – a thoroughly new sensation.

She was also, unexpectedly, rather proud of the kitchen. In an article for *The Lady*, which appeared two months after she had moved in, she was photographed standing in it, quite close to the cooker. She had shown the journalist round the library, the dining room, the patio. He remarked that 'the enormous kitchen, with all its modern equipment, was kept until last'. In 'Moving House'

Daphne described it as one of the nicest rooms at Kilmarth.

One improvement at Daphne's new home was the separate quarters for her family to use on their frequent visits. And the last task of the builders was to convert one of the stone basement rooms into a chapel, reached by a twisting stair from the front hall. Fresh flowers were placed there every week, and a crib at Christmas. She found it soothing, often going down to say a private prayer.

She walked as usual, though this was an entirely different experience from walking at Menabilly. Her usual route took her down – and up – 'Thrombosis Hill', as she quickly dubbed it. She could still swim, at Bewly beach: 'I always feel better afterwards, despite the climb up.' But in the gloom and the rain of her first winter there, she missed Menabilly, mainly because of the lack of suitable walking on the doorstep and the lack of corridors in the house, which had provided covered exercise. Still, the wretched weather provided inspiration for an entertaining piece she wrote for a gift book to be given Prince Philip on his fiftieth birthday, called 'A Winter's Afternoon at Kilmarth': 'Dressed like Tolstoy in his declining years, fur cap with ear flaps, padded jerkin and rubber boots to the knee, I venture forth.'

There were problems about where to settle to write: 'I love the Long Room, and it's OK for the Prince Philip piece, but for a proper story or brew, it's more difficult as there isn't room for a proper desk. I really almost need a Hut!' She thought about Menabilly often, wondering if it had 'reverted to a sort of Rashleigh gloom, with all those frowning portraits on the walls'.

By the spring she was more cheerful. The camellias were out, forsythia was adorning the Long Room, there was a planned trip to Crete with Kits and Hacker (as Olive was now known), and she enjoyed shopping for new clothes amid regrets there was no Marks and Spencer in St Austell. Even if she was not writing, there was always plenty to do, if only dealing with fans – something which Esther began to help more with. Daphne had always been diligent about her correspondence, and courteous: she answered a letter from a reader pointing out some errors in *The House on the Strand* good-naturedly, responding to each of his points and alerting him to her next book, a volume of short stories, due out in July: 'probably *full* of errors but I hope you enjoy them nonetheless'. She had even buried the hatchet with the Rashleighs: she made friends with Philip's new wife, Veronica, and was again walking the paths of Menabilly on her visits.

She enjoyed having her grandchildren to stay – 'She would delight in watching them playing cricket on summer evenings and would sometimes have a bat herself,' said Kits – and the novel she had thought about long ago, about 'the old lady surrounded by a mob of boys' when England is invaded by a foreign power – American Marines landing at Par, as it turned out – began to take shape. The title was '*Rule Britannia*, which rather pleases me – it's very subtle!' (The title she favoured, *The Take-over Bid*, had been taken by someone writing about business tycoons.) Kits's sons Freddie and Robbie would be models for two of the boys, as was her godson Toby, son of her GP, Dr Luther, along with Esther's son, Ralph, who became Terry.

DAPHNE 1946 KITS TEWM FLAVIA [handwritten] DAPHNE, NE), 1976 [handwritten]

LEFT Daphne's daily walks took her down to the sea by means of a steep slope, which she called Thrombosis Hill.
ABOVE Daphne used these matching photographs of herself returning from family excursions to Polridmouth, thirty years apart, on her Christmas card of 1976. ('Track' was one of her nicknames.)

She enjoyed writing about the resistance and the face of Cornwall's proposed development as 'one vast leisure-land' with the proposed construction of a miniature Switzerland out of the white china-clay mountains and training of the unemployed as ski instructors and sleigh drivers. The eccentric ex-actress Mad, living in a house overlooking the sea (just like Daphne), was apparently modelled on – and the book was dedicated to – Gladys Cooper (who died the year before the book was published) but bore a resemblance to Daphne herself:

Emma glanced nervously at her grandmother. At least she hadn't got her peaked cap on, so she didn't look too much

like Mao Tse-tung. Actually, with her white hair brushed upwards like that she looked rather good. Formidable, in fact. On the other hand, it might have been better if she had been dressed to suit her near-eighty years, perhaps in a sensible skirt, and worn a soft cardigan around her shoulders, preferably pale blue, instead of that Robin Hood jerkin with leather sleeves.

Despite the humour, the book was not widely admired. It was to be her last novel (aptly set in Cornwall, just as her first was), though she wrote two biographies, of Francis Bacon and his brother Anthony, *Golden Lads* and *The Winding Stair*. A.L. Rowse was complimentary about *Golden Lads,* saying that she had made a genuine contribution to sixteenth-century English history by her discovery of a previously unknown archive. 'She really worked on them. She didn't just rely on having good researchers.' High praise indeed.

A.L. Rowse still took an interest, coming to lunch – which was

ABOVE Daphne in reflective mood.
OPPOSITE Daphne in active mood: she was fond of swimming all her life.

she will not do it, then she is Madame Non-Non. She always knows her own mind, and it is usually Non.'

This was undoubtedly a sensible decision, devoted though she was to her dogs. She had almost always had West Highland terriers, and in 1976, after Moray died, she acquired two puppies, Mac and Kenzie, named after her favourite Mackenzie whisky, which she used to drink with ginger ale ('whisky and ginger arse-hole,' she used to call it, says Kits) on the dot of 7.30 p.m., before adjourning to the television room for the evening. Whisky with ginger was the luxury she chose when she was the guest on *Desert Island Discs* in 1977. She would have Dubonnet before lunch, always out of the same glass.

Her enthusiasm for television – but, more probably, the fact that Kits was directing – made her agree to a television interview with Cliff Michelmore to mark her seventieth birthday in 1977. It turned out to be an uplifting experience. He took her on a boat in the Fowey harbour, where for the first time in years, she steered: 'It's wonderful to feel my hands on the wheel again. I remember exactly where the channel is, what the tide is doing, where the sandbanks are.' Afterwards, she curled up on the sofa in the Long Room at Kilmarth to talk about the influences on her writing (*Jane Eyre* and *Rebecca*; *Treasure Island* and *Jamaica Inn*; Hemingway and *I'll Never Be Young Again*), the great importance of places, her world of make-believe ('even at my advanced age, I pretend to be someone else') and her remaining ambition, to be a shepherd: 'I have a terrific thing about sheep. I really try to talk to them in their language.'

Mary Luther, a frequent visitor to the house who accompanied her on her long walks, could also testify to that. And in an introduction to a book about eccentrics (never published) written about this time, Daphne wrote of this 'small singularity': 'I converse with sheep in their own language. They understand me. My baa accent is impeccable with the sheep. The ewes look up, and answer. I enquire after their health, and that of their lambs, and

always delicious, he said, and wine was always offered, but never drunk by either. In *Friends and Contemporaries*, he wrote about the inscription she wrote in one of her books: 'For A L, my Professor and dear friend. Madame Non-Non, otherwise Daphne', which referred to 'the game we play since she came to Kilmarth. When her old senior makes suggestions – for example, that she should write a book about her Dogs, as I have done about my Cats – and

KILMARTH: 'THE LAST FRONTIER'

they reply. My accent is not quite so good with the cattle . . .' This was an echo of something she had written a dozen years before in an essay for a book called *What I Believe*. 'Conversing with beast and bird is my way of giving thanks.' If anything would make her believe in God, it was 'watching wildlife in the countryside, a constant miracle, and noting the change in their routine through the four seasons'.

But despite the apparent relaxation of that interview, she was beginning to be gripped by discontent and depression. A trip to Scotland with Kits and Hacker failed to bring her the inspiration she'd hoped for. She was very exercised by the film of *A Bridge Too Far* about the Battle of Arnhem in the Second World War, a failed offensive in which Tommy had played a leading role. She had argued with its director, Richard Attenborough, about the script, which she felt did not pay due respect to Tommy's reservations about the mission, but she failed to get the balance of the film redressed, and remained upset and angry.

BELOW A stone stile on the footpath above Par Sands, one of Daphne's routes.
RIGHT Holding one of her father's walking sticks, and wearing the cap she favoured in later years, Daphne stands at the top of Thrombosis Hill.

DAPHNE DU MAURIER AT HOME

KILMARTH: 'THE LAST FRONTIER'

To add to the cauldron of emotions, she had been persuaded that she should write an autobiography, a book on the making of a writer, which involved delving back into her childhood. This caused some angst, but she felt that if anchored to places, it might succeed: 'I must base it on something – like houses, and the influence they have on one's development.' She remembered 'very vividly' Cumberland Terrace and Cannon Hall, but credited also the other houses where she was taken by her parents – especially 'that great house Milton, belonging to the Fitzwilliams, where I stayed, aged eleven, and never forgot, and which was really the Rebecca house, more than Mena'.

She found the necessary self-examination difficult and sometimes painful. When Sheila Hodges asked her to say something about the process of identification she mused, 'I can't say precisely at what given moment I am identifying, or with which characters, but of course it is always easier when writing in the first person and when that person can be identified with a house.'

Her title of *Growing Pains: The Shaping of a Writer* was disliked by the American publishers – it sounded too much like period pains to them – and the book was renamed *Myself When Young*, the title it now has. A.L. Rowse was impressed with a book that said so much about the inspiration of a writer, describing how 'The seed of an idea might take some five-and-twenty years or more to germinate and come to the surface, fusing with later observations – these observations in their turn blending with characters from long-forgotten books; but finally a story of a novel would emerge, and neither the model nor the writer would be aware of the transformation or of its origins.'

'In fact,' he added, 'a curious thing happened, she told me, after writing this book. Hitherto she had always projected herself into the character she was writing about and became that person, woman or man. She feels that writing about herself directly "did something" to her, inhibited the creative process from operating. She never wrote another novel.'

Daphne with Mac and Kenzie, her two West Highland terriers – her favourite breed.

She never wrote another book. In 1981, *The Rebecca Notebook*, her actual notebook for the novel, which had been used as evidence in the trial for plagiarism, was published, along with a collection of articles and essays that had appeared elsewhere. Rowse quoted her as calling it 'with her usual candour "scraping the barrel"'. But that was it. In the cheery interview with Wilfred De'ath ten years before, she had said firmly: 'I believe writing's a thing you can go on doing. Right up to 80. Look at Agatha Christie!' But after her seventieth birthday she didn't write anything more. For Daphne, whose life was completely focused on the need to write, the need to create other worlds, this was calamitous; it took away the meaning for existence. Though she carried on with her 'routes', she never found another source of inspiration. She continued to read widely, always the newspapers in the morning, magazines and books – though Flavia said that in her last years she read only Jane Austen – but the creativity she had always relied upon was now silent. She was involved with one more book, *Enchanted Cornwall: Her Pictorial Memoir* (published after her death), in which extracts from her books and essays are cunningly interwoven and interspersed with photographs of the settings. It is, as Daphne's foreword puts it, a 'pleasing tapestry'. Her foreword also contains a passage, echoing her writing elsewhere, that has become indelibly associated with her love for Cornwall: 'I walked this land with a dreamer's freedom and with a waking man's perception – places, houses whispered to me their secrets and shared with me their sorrows and their joys. And in return I gave them something of myself, a few of my novels passing into the folk-lore of this ancient place.'

Her remaining years were dogged by depression, ill health and inability to write. In 1981, after an attempt at suicide – she had taken too few tablets to have an effect – a rota of nurses was set up to allow her to continue living at Kilmarth. One poignant vignette is of her early evening ritual of rolling a ball for her dogs along the Long Room, although, oddly, only Mac was allowed to fetch the ball: Kenzie she kept by her side. That was her time for playing the tapes of American singers – Frank Sinatra, Nat King Cole, Perry Como – that had been specially recorded by Kits. There were many such efforts to cheer her. Once Esther arranged for her to meet Val Doonican, whom Daphne also liked, when he was performing locally. But nothing could alter the state she was now in.

The pattern of her life had changed for ever. Daphne, who had so loved solitude, was now always accompanied by nurses and companions. Jennette Martin felt herself very fortunate to be one of those companions: 'I was in seventh heaven, working for someone I looked up to. She was one of my favourite authors, and I was surrounded by all those books and images, her personal pictures and portraits. I did feel privileged.'

Her memories are rather fond ones: of taking up Daphne's breakfast on a tray, with the very old china cafetière; of arranging the cushions on the sofa – 'there were loads of them, about 20, and they had to be arranged in a certain way – that was a quite a challenge'; of helping Daphne with the crossword. 'There was sometimes conversation. She didn't give a lot away, she was quite self-contained, but she had a sense of humour.'

There might be a walk on Par Beach in the morning. 'She would always walk the same distance, every day, and then back.' Sometimes there would be visits to the hairdresser, or Jennette might drive her over to see Angela, and in the evenings there was television. But the television would go off at 10.30 p.m., whatever the programme; routine was more important than knowing the ending of a story. 'It was something that struck me as unusual for someone so intelligent. She would say, "We'll never know." It seemed surprising, especially for a writer. Perhaps she made up her own endings . . .'

At the beginning of 1989, Daphne began to give up eating. Then in mid-April, she made a series of visits on unscheduled days to friends and relatives – her sister Angela, Veronica Rashleigh – and to Polridmouth Beach. On 18 April she rang Oriel unexpectedly. In the conversation she said, 'I went down to the chapel today, and said a prayer for you.' On 19 April 1989, the nurse took up her breakfast tray and found that she had died in her sleep.

CHAPTER 9
THE LEGACY

Daphne's funeral was as muted as her life had been in her last few years. The service was at Tregaminion Chapel, the tiny church on Menabilly land – and, fittingly, the only spot from which one can now catch a proper glimpse of the house that held Daphne's heart. It was a small affair, though the Queen Mother sent a wreath of freesias, carnations, lilies and tulips 'in affectionate remembrance'. Apart from her family – her sisters, children and grandchildren – there was a handful of friends. Canon Michael Oatey, vicar of Tywardreath, who had known her for fourteen years, led the service. Grandson Freddie read the joyous poem 'Everyone Sang' by Siegfried Sassoon, and granddaughter Grace read the verse from *Cymbeline* that had given Daphne the title for her biography, *Golden Lads*. The cremation was at Glyn Valley Crematorium in Bodmin. She had once picked the spot at Menabilly where she wanted to be buried, but now, as she had requested, her ashes were 'put to cliff' ('a Cornish expression she enjoyed', said Kits) and scattered near Kilmarth, by a standing stone that was (though no longer) close by her old walking route.

The auction of Daphne's possessions was rather less subdued: her fans turned out in force. Her 'Sheraton Revival writing desk, top with inset leather and easel, central section, two long and two short fitted drawers and tapered square legs, terminating in castors', as described in the catalogue, was expected to fetch £800–£1,200. In fact, the owners of Jamaica Inn bought it for over £8,000, for their Daphne du Maurier Room, which opened the following year. Kilmarth was returned to the Rashleighs, who sold it: it has been extensively refurbished and embellished by its new owner.

There had been many appreciative obituaries, one of which, by Margaret Forster in *The Times,* was so effective that she was commissioned to write a biography. It was authorized by the family, by then formed into the Chichester Partnership (the name came from the family code: if the family wanted to talk about someone present or nearby without their realizing, the subject of the conversation would be 'Mrs Chichester'), though they had reservations about the result, feeling that too much had been made of her close relationships with women and that Daphne's sense of humour had been largely missed. It remains the most thorough account of Daphne's life and works.

Daphne's ashes were scattered close to Kilmarth beside this (now removed) standing stone on one of her favourite routes.

Shelves of Daphne du Maurier novels in Bookends, the specialist bookshop in Fowey.

It was not the first biography to appear – indeed in the two years that followed Daphne's death no fewer than six books about Daphne were apparently vying with each other. It is a prospect that on one level might have reassured Daphne – her position in the literary canon was obviously secure – but on another would have appalled her. This intensely private and retiring person was about to have her life picked over in minute and sometimes biased detail. The first book to make it into print was by a fan, Martyn Shallcross, who had made friends with her in her last years and considered that he was best placed to present her to the world, citing conversations with her, along with photographs of himself with her, arm about her waist. Judith Cook, who had known Daphne and Tommy in the 1960s and had visited them at Menabilly, was second in line, but the one by Jeanne's formidable partner Noel Welch in co-operation with Sheila Hodges fell by the wayside. Sheila Hodges's account of her experience of editing

Daphne appeared later in an article for *Women's History Review* in 2002 and was included in *The Daphne du Maurier Companion*, edited by Helen Taylor, published in 2007 to mark the centenary of Daphne's birth. Oriel Malet's illuminating *Letters from Menabilly*, a collection of letters from over thirty years, came out in 1993.

The biography by Margaret Forster also appeared in 1993. It was she who, through her husband Hunter Davies's recommendation of a publisher, midwifed the most insightful book, *Daphne du Maurier: A Daughter's Memoir*: Flavia's vivid and affectionate account of life at Menabilly was published the following year. During the wide-ranging coverage, Flavia asked Sir Richard

Rashleigh, who had inherited Menabilly in 1988, if she could have a photograph taken at Menabilly. Permission was granted, but when she turned up with a photographer, they were escorted off the land – *she* had been given permission, she was told, not the photographer. However, he allowed photographs of the three siblings there in the centenary year of Daphne's birth.

Other books began to appear, many of them novels inspired by her most famous book, including *Mrs de Winter* by Susan Hill; *The Other Rebecca* by Maureen Freely; *Rebecca's Tale* by Sally Beauman; and *The Key to Rebecca* by Ken Follett, in which a copy of the novel was used for encryption. Mrs Danvers began to develop a life of her own, featuring in books by Stephen King and Jasper Fforde. More adaptations of *Rebecca* were made, including, in 2006, a musical version staged in Vienna and then in other European cities and in Japan.

Critical analyses of Daphne's work appeared, such as *Daphne du Maurier: Haunted Heiress* by Nina Auerbach and *Daphne du Maurier: Writing, Identity and the Gothic Imagination*. Her work was studied on literature courses, and became the subject of PhD theses and learned papers. For example, 'A Little Strain with Servants' dealt with 'gender, modernity and domesticity', discussing the servant–mistress relationship in *Rebecca* in a 'part social survey and part imaginative recreation of the world of domestic service' and producing a 'quasi-socialist and quasi-Freudian reading of the relations between women' (which, despite such language, is informative about attitudes to servants at the time *Rebecca* was written). An international conference to mark the centenary of her birth heard papers on the psychogeography of *Castle Dor*, the ethics of female beauty, Cornish nationalism, and *Rebecca* and family therapy. It was all rather different to the critical reaction in her lifetime. 'She would, I think, be at once pleased and sardonically amused, that her work is being studied in literature courses at universities all over the world, and scrutinised from every literary and psychological angle,' said Sheila Hodges.

There were less academic but no less enthusiastic homages by individuals, some of whose research had deep roots. In 1950, Stanley and Joy Vickers had spent their honeymoon in Looe, and were taken 'on a sea trip round to the River Fowey and up to Lerryn, passing on the way the du Maurier home at Ferryside'. Thus began their 'lifelong interest'. They started collecting and cataloguing books of the whole family, eventually published as *The du Maurier Companion*, its aim being to 'share an inexhaustible fund of memories coloured throughout by the du Maurier family'.

Collin Langley came to her work rather late when, during a family holiday on Bodmin Moor, he visited Jamaica Inn and bought the book: 'My sister-in-law bought *Rebecca*; so I read them both, and I was hooked.' He went to Fowey for the first time in 1999, and, by chance, stayed at the Old Ferry Inn. 'I didn't know the significance of the Ferry Inn!' After he retired from his job as a tax advisor, he decided to put his research skills to a different use and explore her interest in music, giving a presentation at the centenary conference in 2007. He moved on to her poetry and then, after a conversation with Kits in which Kits said 'Nobody has captured her sense of humour', he started his next project, reading many books on the psychology of humour. He is intensely engaged with his chosen subjects: 'Helen Taylor calls me an independent scholar.' The results of his research – 'The Appeal of Poets and Poetry' and 'But the Laughter Lingers', as well as 'The Mystery of Daphne's Music Unravelled' – are all now in the Daphne du Maurier archive at the University of Exeter.

Appropriately for an author known for her 'sense of place', interest in the area Daphne had immortalized in her novels flourished. In 1992, a guided walk on 'Daphne du Maurier Connections', starting at Menabilly Barton, attracted seventy fans. It was the brainchild of Lynn Goold, a Blue Badge guide, who had visited Kilmarth as a child, waiting in the car as her father, a clock-maker and jeweller, cleaned the clocks. 'I had always been aware of Daphne du Maurier – the newsagent in Par used to sell her books and she would go in there to sign them. But it was only later that I appreciated just how much she had written about the area I was passionate about, about the places where I used to go walking.'

More guided trips, angled towards the landscapes of the books, followed and in the course of these Lynn met Ella Westland, a lecturer at the University of Exeter. Together they became enthusiastic about promoting walks and talks about the author. As it happened, the local council had a similar idea. Eager to boost visitor numbers in a slack part of the year – the 'tourist dip' between Easter and Regatta Week in high summer – the council lighted on the idea of a festival in May for Daphne du Maurier. Conveniently, this coincided with her birthday.

It was a period when, nationwide, literary tourism, exploiting readers' interest in their favourite authors, was booming. The Brontës, Catherine Cookson, Thomas Hardy all were graced with their own patch of Britain. On the other side of Cornwall was Poldark Country, popularized by Howard Spring's books. So the signs went up for Du Maurier Country, leaflets were produced on 'Daphne du Maurier in Cornwall', and Devon and Cornwall Overseas Marketing (DACOM) was established in 1995, to promulgate the efficacy of events-led tourism to attract visitors out of season.

One example of this was the first Daphne du Maurier Literary Festival, announced for 1997, the ninetieth anniversary of her birth – rather to the surprise of her family. But they gave their blessing and Kits Browning in particular, based as he is at Ferryside, has continued to be involved. That year Lynn Goold

Menabilly Lodge, Fowey

Tristan's stone, which once marked the burial place of King Mark's son at Castle Dore, stood for many years at Four Turnings by the drive to Menabilly.

opened the Daphne du Maurier Literary Centre. The back room of the centre is a work of art in itself, with storyboards and pictures illustrating the Cornish novels. (*My Cousin Rachel* is illustrated by a photograph of the thatched Menabilly Lodge at Four Turnings with the original wrought-iron gates of Menabilly and Tristan's stone, all as Daphne and Angela must have seen them on their first exploration.)

Visitors can watch a video about Daphne, see a collection of her books in different languages, and leaf through the thick file of cuttings, including the charming 'Introduction to Fowey' (illustrated by Mabel Lucie Attwell) written by Daphne for a publicity booklet issued by the Chamber of Commerce:

Wherever he wanders, the visitor will be aware of this fact that Fowey is first and foremost a sea-port, and if he has a spark of imagination he will want to get himself upon the water . . . Once afloat, the visitor will seek no other form of amusement. Let others drive their fifty miles or even five, he wisely lets his car remain in a garage (it is madness to bring it down into the narrow streets anyway) and enjoys, like Mr Rat and Mr Mole, the incomparable thrill of 'messing about in boats' . . . He soon realises that Fowey has a magic all her own, and surely one of the most haunting memories he and his family take home with them will be the sound of a ship's siren, deep and low, and the thrash of her propellers, as she bears down harbour outward bound.

Glass cabinets display items belonging to Daphne such as her plaid shirt and one of her treasured belts. A letter written to Leo Walmsley, when he was ill, recommended a 'rib-shaking' book' which turns out to be *Lucky Jim* by Kingsley Amis, and Daphne added: '*One Fat Englishman* made me sick with laughter.' She also recommended Peter Cheyney stories. It was a letter written not long before he died – Daphne had, with typical generosity, quietly paid for a private room at the Truro hospital for him. There are mementoes of the first du Maurier festival: a souvenir cover of the first programme, which took place on the croquet lawn at Fowey Hall Hotel, and a bottle of the Reserve Claret Bordeaux labelled specially. The most popular event that first year was the one-man show given by the actor Sir John Mills, followed by the jazz musician George Melly and crime authors P.D. James and Ruth Rendell in conversation. Their presence reflects the intention from the beginning that the festival would not confine itself exclusively to the local author. Within a year it had established itself as a major arts and literary festival, as Jonathan Aberdeen, director from the start, pointed out, with its blend of 'local community

events and strong performers like Sir John Mills' (who returned twice more). It is still going strong and attracting visitors from far afield (one year 200 Germans chartered a plane from Hamburg), despite the trials imposed by switches from local to county council, and recession: in 2011, the du Maurier Festival Society was set up, with a Friends and Patrons scheme – though in 2013, the name changed, and the du Maurier Festival Society is billed as presenting the Fowey Festival of Words and Music.

The main attraction for many visitors remains Daphne du Maurier. Key to that is the involvement of the University of Exeter, which has an archive of du Maurier family papers. Now, linked to the main festival, the Tremough Campus Culture Festival takes place at the Cornwall campus of the University – which in 2008 named its main building after Daphne (another sign of recognition which might have surprised her). Helen Taylor, Professor of English at the University of Exeter, was drawn in by Ella Westland and has helped organize every festival since. Presciently, she had – on a holiday in Fowey years ago – stayed at 8 Readymoney Cove, renting a flat at the top of the house. 'I actually slept in the room Daphne du Maurier wrote in,' she said, 'and I didn't know.'

Each of Daphne's children has taken part at some point, and in 2007, the centenary of Daphne's birth, Tessa, Flavia and Kits all appeared on stage together. The 2011 festival focused on a triumphant discovery of the short story 'The Doll', the culmination of a long search by Ann Willmore, owner of the Fowey bookshop, Bookends: she had tracked it down in a collection of previously unpublished short stories called *The Editor Regrets*. In 2012, the focus was a preview of the film of *The Scapegoat*.

Over the years there have been varied and imaginative ways of exploiting Daphne's life and work: an exhibition of her paintings, readings of her stories at the linked library festival, boat trips re-enacting the early morning boat ride to the church in Lanteglos for her marriage. Plays of her novels have been staged

ABOVE AND RIGHT A surprising exhibition at the 2011 du Maurier Festival showed pictures Daphne had painted in a brief period in the 1950s, including a chateau as in *The Scapegoat,* and the French cottages that later featured in her 1963 novel *The Glass-Blowers.*

in appropriate locations by the Tywardreath Players: *Rebecca* in a marquee at Menabilly Barton; *The House on the Strand* in Marsh Villa Gardens, bordered on one side by the tunnel of the Paddington-to-Penzance railway tunnel (with the train emerging at a well-timed and significant moment); and a rain-drenched rendition of *Frenchman's Creek* in Pont Pill.

Most of the festival, however, takes place in the Festival Village, a set of marquees, large and small, on the sports field of the community college, conveniently close to the Fowey Hall Hotel with its box of fishing nets and beach clobber on one side of the porch and a row of wellington boots lined up in order of size on the other side. Some more intimate events take place in its billiards room, but other events are held in the town hall or in St Fimbarrus' parish church – or even on the town quay, where, in 2012, the Champagne Cornwall Chorus, undaunted by the chill and fresh from winning medals, sang with brio.

The town quay is the final destination of Lynn Goold's walk around 'Daphne du Maurier's Fowey', perhaps the best way to get a sense of the author's home ground. She starts by taking the literary pilgrim along Hanson Drive to the corner of Pike's Hill, from which one can see up Pont Pill, scene of the wrecked *Jane Slade* which inspired Daphne's first book. Just peeking out over the smooth roundness of the hill above Pont Pill was the tower of St Wyllow's Church where she married Tommy. A little further along, she stops to indicate the rocks below St Catherine's Castle, over which Dona St Columb (rather improbably) ran in *Frenchman's Creek.* Then Lynn guides her flock down a pretty lane running alongside the Readymoney home to Point Neptune, which has what were thought to be (but Lynn is not so sure) the original gates from Menabilly. Along the Esplanade she points out Q's home, The Haven, where Daphne used to go for Sunday suppers, and the school that Tessa and Flavia briefly attended. In front of St Fimbarrus' Church, she gathers people to tell them about the site of a long-demolished pub, the Rose and Crown, the back room of which was the place of assignation between Rachel and Rainaldi in *My Cousin Rachel.* And, a few steps away, at the town quay she points out Daphne's first home in Fowey, Ferryside.

The alert can spot homages to Daphne everywhere, from the window of Bookends – which, during the festival, is a paean of praise with old adverts for her 'new' novel *The Scapegoat*, a *Woman's Journal* of March 1966 proclaiming Daphne du Maurier's newest suspense story ('The Breakthrough') and memorabilia of du Maurier stamps, thimbles and mugs – to the pretty fully furnished bus shelter on the outskirts of Fowey, with its painting and inscription of the famous first sentence of *Rebecca*.

Daphne never owned a house – apart from her wedding present of Cannon Hall Cottage, but that reverted to her mother after her father's death. And not one of the houses Daphne lived in is open to the public, though the house at Readymoney was put up for sale in 2011 – for £1.7 million. (It remained on sale for a long time.) A plaque on the wall notes Daphne's brief residence.

However, walking in the footsteps of Daphne is something that one may easily do, for this is her town, her countryside. Even something as simple as taking a trip across the river to Bodinnick – the journey she took so often – and walking up the hill to the Old Ferry Inn can bring a sense of the young author on the brink of her career. The crossing is by a solid, stable car ferry now, run by Toms, who took over the old Slade boatyard.

One can walk up to the Gribbin, as she did so often: past Coombe Farm where Ron Diggens used to land his aeroplane, and alongside Polridmouth Beach where one can, thrillingly, pass Rebecca's boathouse. Except of course it's not. It's a solid stone house, once a mill house. But that is the twist: there's a sense of fiction taking over from reality. Daphne was a novelist, a weaver of dreams. This is not, and wasn't, a boathouse. Polridmouth Cottage is now a holiday let, along with Keeper's Cottage, once Southcott Cottage and the home of Miss Willcox and Miss Phillips, originals of the sisters in 'Don't Look Now'. Both are available to be rented from Menabilly Holidays, whose website studiously avoids any direct mention of Daphne du Maurier. For Menabilly, inhabited by Rashleighs again, has withdrawn into seclusion. The Rashleighs are reluctant to exploit any association – though they recognize the part she played in the history of the house: Kits reported Sir Richard's comment to him once, 'God sent her. Because if she hadn't lived there, the house would have fallen down.'

Perhaps guests are drawn to Polridmouth Cottage because of the Daphne connection – though the house owes more to Ron Diggens, its long-term tenant, than to Daphne, and the logbook inside, filled with comments from loyal returning visitors, makes barely a mention of her. None of her novels is on the bookshelves. (There is one book, *What is at Stake and Why Not Say So* by C.E.M. Joad, which has the bookplate of Ron Diggens inside.)

A greater sense of Daphne can be gleaned from Cuckoo Cottage at Frenchman's Creek – though that had nothing to do with her. Here in the location that entranced her are plenty of Daphne-related books, and a logbook with tributes to her, along with sightings – of birds, including 'a lone mute swan (ghost of Dona St Columb perhaps)' – and accounts of the re-enactment of the story set in the creek.

There can never be an actual house for Daphne du Maurier, as there is a Brontë Parsonage, a Bateman's for Kipling, a Greenway for Agatha Christie. The place to find out about her houses is her writing. As she made evident in *Growing Pains*, the houses she lived in gave her a bond with the past, nurturing and inspiring her imagination. Just as, she points out, the houses we have known can perhaps inspire ours:

Who can ever affirm, or deny, that the houses which have sheltered us as children, or as adults, and our predecessors too, do not have embedded in their walls, one with dust and cobwebs, one with the overlay of fresh wallpaper and paint, the imprint of what-has-been, the suffering, the joy? We are all ghosts of yesterday, and the phantom of tomorrow awaits us alike in sunshine or in shadow, dimly perceived at times, never lost.

SELECT BIBLIOGRAPHY

Cook, Judith, *Daphne: Portrait of Daphne du Maurier* (Bantam Press, 1991)

Doe, Helen, *Jane Slade of Polruan: The Inspiration for Daphne du Maurier's First Novel* (Truran, 2002)

du Maurier, Angela, *It's Only the Sister* (Peter Davies, 1951)

—, *Old Maids Remember* (Peter Davies, 1966)

du Maurier, Daphne (most of her books are now published by Virago):

—, *The Loving Spirit* (Heinemann, 1932)

—, *I'll Never Be Young Again* (Heinemann, 1933)

—, *The Progress of Julius* (Heinemann, 1933)

—, *Gerald: A Portrait* (Gollancz, 1933)

—, *Jamaica Inn* (Gollancz, 1936)

—, *The Du Mauriers* (Gollancz, 1937)

—, *Rebecca* (Gollancz, 1938)

—, *Come Wind, Come Weather* (Heinemann, 1940)

—, *Frenchman's Creek* (Gollancz, 1941)

—, *The Hungry Hill* (Gollancz, 1943)

—, *The Years Between* (Gollancz, 1945)

—, *The King's General* (Gollancz, 1946)

—, *September Tide* (Gollancz, 1949)

—, *The Parasites* (Gollancz, 1949)

—, *My Cousin Rachel* (Gollancz, 1951)

—, *The Apple Tree* (Gollancz, 1952)

—, *Mary Anne* (Gollancz, 1954)

—, *The Scapegoat* (Gollancz, 1957)

—, *The Infernal World of Branwell Brontë* (Gollancz, 1960)

— (with Sir Arthur Quiller-Couch), *Castle Dor* (Dent, 1962)

—, *The Glass-Blowers* (Gollancz, 1963)

—, *The Flight of the Falcon* (Gollancz, 1965)

—, *Vanishing Cornwall* (Gollancz, 1967)

—, *The House on the Strand* (Gollancz, 1967)

—, *Not After Midnight: And Other Stories* (including 'Don't Look Now') (Gollancz, 1971)

—, *Rule Britannia* (Gollancz, 1972)

—, *The Golden Lads* (Gollancz, 1975)

—, *The Winding Stair* (Gollancz, 1976)

—, *Growing Pains: The Shaping of a Writer* (Gollancz, 1979), later retitled *Myself When Young*

—, *The Rebecca Notebook and Other Memories* (Gollancz, 1981)

—, *Enchanted Cornwall: Her Pictorial Memoir*, ed. Piers Dudgeon (Michael Joseph, 1989)

—, *The Doll: Short Stories* (Virago, 2011)

Forster, Margaret, *Daphne du Maurier* (Chatto and Windus, 1993)

Jacob, Valerie, *From Tregonissey to Trenarren: the Cornish Years of A.L. Rowse* (St Austell, 2001)

Keast, John, *The Story of Fowey* (Dyllansow Truran, 1983)

Leng, Flavia, *Daphne du Maurier: A Daughter's Memoir* (Mainstream, 1994)

Malet, Oriel, *Letters from Menabilly* (Weidenfeld and Nicholson, 1993)

Mead, Richard, *General 'Boy': The Life of Sir Frederick Browning* (Pen and Sword, 2010)

Ollard, Richard (ed.), *The Diaries of A.L. Rowse* (Allen Lane, 2003)

Payton, Philip, *A.L. Rowse and Cornwall* (University of Exeter Press, 2005)

Quiller-Couch, Sir Arthur, *The Astonishing History of Troytown* (Cassell, 1888)

Rowse, A.L., *Friends and Contemporaries* (Methuen, 1989)

Taylor, Helen (ed.), *The Daphne du Maurier Companion* (Virago, 2007)

Vickers, Stanley, *The du Maurier Companion* (Fowey Rare Books, 1997)

Vyvyan, Clara, *Letters from a Cornish Garden* (Michael Joseph, 1972)

—, *The Helford River* (Peter Owen, 1956)

Williams, Michael (ed.), *The Cornish World of Daphne du Maurier* (Bossiney Books, 1995)

Extracts from titles by Daphne du Maurier reproduced with permission of Curtis Brown Group Ltd, London on behalf of The Chichester Partnership.

FURTHER INFORMATION

Daphne du Maurier Literary Centre and Tourist
Information
5 South Street
Fowey
Cornwall
PL23 1AR
tel. 01726 833616

Bookends of Fowey
4 South Street, Fowey PL23 1AR
tel. 01726 833361

Bookends Too
25a Fore Street
PL23 1AH
tel. 01726 832595
www.bookendsoffowey.com

Frenchman's Creek can be rented from:
The Landmark Trust
Shottesbrooke
Maidenhead
Berkshire
SL6 3SW
tel. 01628 825925
www.landmarktrust.org.uk

Jamaica Inn
Bolventor
Launceston
Cornwall PL15 7TS
tel. 01566 86250
www.jamaicainn.co.uk

Menabilly Holidays
Menabilly
Par
Cornwall PL24 2TN
tel. 01726 808150
www.menabilly.com

Lanhydrock
Bodmin
PL30 5AD
tel. 01208 265950
www.nationaltrust.org.uk/lanhydrock

OTHER USEFUL WEBSITES

www.dumaurier.org

The Daphne du Maurier Festival is now the
Fowey Festival of Words and Music
www.foweyfestival.com

Almost all Daphne du Maurier's works are
published by Virago
www.virago.co.uk

Information about Langley End can be found on
www.prestonherts.co.uk

Information about Milton can be found at
www.thearchive.org.uk

Interviews with Daphne du Maurier – from the
BBC archive and online – can be seen at
www.bbc.co.uk/archive/writers/12222.shtml

www.cornwalls.co.uk

A link to the interview with Daphne du Maurier
by Orson Welles can be found at
www.old radioworld.com

www.fowey.co.uk

www.visit-fowey.com

www.foweyheritage.co.uk

www.visitcornwall.co.uk

www.cornwalls.co.uk/Fowey

www.tywardreath.org.uk

www.polruan.org.uk

www.quillercouch.co.uk

INDEX

Numbers in *italics* refer to illustrations

ACKNOWLEDGMENTS

This book would not have been possible, nor such a pleasure, without the generous help of Daphne's children – Tessa, Flavia and Kits. I much enjoyed my meetings with them to look through their photographs and to hear their memories of their homes. Thanks too to Felicity Blunt and Becky Ritchie of Curtis Brown.

This project was first thought of in early 2010, and the interest of Sue and Charles Sandison led to an invitation to join them at the Fowey Royal Regatta that summer. And so I started my explorations with them – glimpsing some of Daphne's homes, and walking along the coast to Polridmouth Beach to see for the first time the building that inspired Rebecca's boathouse, now a holiday cottage to which we all returned to stay in 2012. Eileen Cox and her friend Chrissie le Marchant, Blue Badge guides both, also joined us there. Their involvement – and loan of material – was much appreciated. Katherine Oakes and David Dawson of the Landmark Trust later enabled me to stay at Frenchman's Creek, another evocative location favoured by Daphne.

In Fowey itself I had friendly assistance from Lynn Goold of the Daphne du Maurier Literary Centre, with its treasure trove of information, and also from her assistant Shirley Johnson. Lynn introduced me to Jennette Martin, who gave me a valuable insight into Daphne's last years. I was glad to meet Ann Willmore of Bookends and David Willmore of Bookends Too – both shops providing excellent sources of books by and about Daphne, and about Cornwall. David Rowan, who played in the grounds of Menabilly as a boy, and Mary Luther, now curator of Fowey Museum, had interesting stories to tell.

One highlight of my research was meeting Esther Rowe, for thirty years housekeeper for Daphne, as well as her son Ralph and her partner Denis Drew, all of whom shed light on Daphne's homes.

I'd like to thank Professor Helen Taylor for her observations on literary tourism and the annual festival, in which she has long been involved, as has Jonathan Aberdeen, its director. Christine Faunch and her staff at the University of Exeter's Special Collections made my research there pleasurable. The National Maritime Museum library staff helped at a crucial point.

Barry Edwards lent me several books; Martin Yates tracked down original Penguin editions of du Maurier's work for me; Collin Langley provided me with the results of his research in Daphne's humour and her love of music.

The great thing about writing for Frances Lincoln is the knowledge that the book will be well tended. So thanks and much appreciation to Andrew Dunn, who commissioned this book; editor Anne Askwith; designer Arianna Osti; and proofreader Nancy Marten.

None of this would have had as much value without the support of Anna and Judith, and especially of Michael, who not only shared in some of the research but had to read and comment on all the chapters. Luckily, he too shares my interest in domestic issues.

PICTURE CREDITS